The Language
of Medicine
in English

REVISED EDITION

The Language of Medicine in English

ETHEL TIERSKY

MARTIN TIERSKY

Medical Consultants

Shirley Lovett, M.D.

Jean Weimer, M.A., R.N.

PRENTICE HALL REGENTS, Englewood Cliffs, New Jersey 07632

Library of Congress Cataloging-in-Publication Data

Tiersky, Ethel, date.
   The language of medicine in English / Ethel Tiersky, Martin
Tiersky ; medical consultants, Shirley Lovett, Jean Weimer — Rev. ed.
   Includes index.
   ISBN 0-13-521444-0
   1. Readers — Medicine.   2. Medicine — Vocabulary — Problems,
exercises, etc.   3. English language — Textbooks for foreign
speakers.   4. English language — Medical English.   I. Tiersky,
Martin, 1935- .   II. Title.
   [DNLM: 1. Nomenclature — problems.   W 15 T564L]
PE1127.M4T54   1992
428.6'4'02461 — dc20
                                                    91–39488
                                                       CIP

Acquisitions editor: *Anne Riddick*
Editorial/production supervision, interior design,
      and photo research: *Louise B. Capuano*
Cover design: *Marianne Frasco*
Pre-press buyer: *Ray Keating*
Manufacturing buyer: *Lori Bulwin*
Scheduler: *Leslie Coward*

©1992 by Prentice Hall Regents
Prentice-Hall, Inc.
A Paramount Communications Company
Englewood Cliffs, New Jersey 07632

Printed in the United States of America

10

ISBN   0-13-521444-0

The *caduceus,* the winged staff with two snakes wrapped around it, is the symbol of the U.S. Army Medical Corps, and it is also commonly used to symbolize the entire medical profession.

The caduceus comes from ancient Roman mythology. It was the magic wand of the god Mercury, who could control the living and the dead with it. The snake was the ancient symbol of health because it could shed its skin and look young again.

Contents

Foreword

This book serves a dual purpose: to give students of English an introduction to the English terminology of medicine and to improve their overall use of the language. *The Language of Medicine in English* is intended for students at the high intermediate or advanced level who are acquainted with the common structural patterns of the language. The principal goals of the learners should be mastering specific vocabulary and idioms and improving their ability to communicate in English, especially with reference to a particular area of work.

The Language of Medicine in English deals with such topics as human anatomy, surgery, medical specialties, and first aid, making it a broad survey of the opportunities and problems inherent in the world of medicine.

Following the text of each chapter is a glossary of 20 special terms (medical vocabulary words and phrases) in which specific technical words and expressions are defined. That is followed by a vocabulary practice section consisting of 15 questions about the vocabulary to reinforce the student's familiarity with the terms.

This revised edition of *The Language of Medicine in English* offers somewhat longer reading sections with numbered paragraphs for easier reference in the exercises. The special terms are boldfaced so that students can easily locate them and study them in context.

In this edition, the exercises have been greatly expanded, introducing work on pronunciation, word parts, and reading skills. Section I—Discussing Medical Matters—includes some questions that ask students to summarize material from the chapter and other questions that ask about personal experiences and opinions. Section II—Analyzing Words and Word Parts—has information and questions about prefixes, roots, suffixes, inflected forms, and multiple meanings of words introduced in the chapter. Section III—Pronouncing Medical and General Words—gives rules and provides drills in pronunciation of the vocabulary used in the chapter. Stress marks and IPA (International Phonetic Alphabet) symbols are used to assist students in learning the pronunciation. Section IV—Using New Words and Phrases—provides practice in using the 20 vocabulary words plus additional medical and general vocabulary from the chapter. Finally, Section V—Checking Comprehension—asks specific questions which require an understanding of the chapter's content to answer. Often, students are referred to specific paragraphs, which they must reread and analyze. The questions in this last section emphasize four important reading skills: determining meaning from context, understanding inferences, grasping main ideas, and recognizing significant supporting details. Following Chapters 5 and 9, there are review exercises.

We hope that by reading the text, studying the vocabulary, and doing the exercises the reader can get a good start toward a successful career in a rewarding medical field.

Our thanks to our consultants: Dr. Shirley Lovett, who practices medicine in Chicago, Illinois, and Mrs. Jean Weimer, professor of nursing and chairperson of the Nursing Department at Harry S Truman College in Chicago. Their expert advice has been invaluable. Thanks also to our editors, Anne Riddick and Kathy Sands Boehmer, whose assistance also enhanced the quality of the text.

Ethel and Martin Tiersky

The Language
of Medicine
in English

CHAPTER 1

Highlights from the History of Medicine

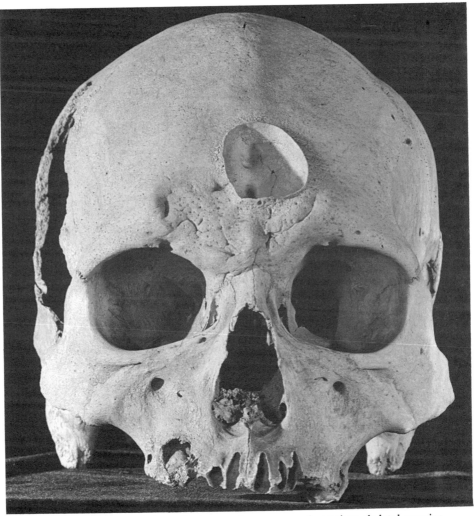

The surgical procedure called *trephining* can be seen even in ancient skeletal remains. *(Neg. #283253, Courtesy Department of Library Services, American Museum of Natural History)*

1.   The practice of medicine is one of the oldest professions in the history of mankind. Some of the methods that ancient healers employed in their efforts to prevent or cure disease are a source of amusement to modern health care workers. However, it is surprising how many medical ideas, techniques, and medications still used today originated in civilizations hundreds and even thousands of years old.

2.   In ancient civilizations, people believed that illnesses were caused either by angry gods or evil spirits, so the earliest "cures" were techniques for pacifying the gods or driving away demons. The use of charms, spells, and prayers was common. Specific foods were also prescribed — a lion's heart to fortify one's courage, or a leaf that resembled a particular body organ to **heal** an affliction of the look-alike body part.

3.   In early societies as in the present day, medical advice came not only from those designated as healers, but from the folk wisdom handed down from one generation to the next. What would cure the common cold? Folk medicine prescribed a dirty sock around the neck. Afflicted with leg cramps? Folk culture cured the condition with a pair of shoes placed upside down under the bed. Tobacco juice was reputed to heal an earache, and black pepper and lard were supposed to cure asthma. Folklore was also full of warnings. Pregnant women, for example, were advised not to hang clothes on a clothesline because this action might produce knots in the umbilical cord.

4.   But prehistoric and ancient peoples also made some medical discoveries of curative value. For example, thousands of years ago, people used willow bark (which contained chemicals similar to those in today's aspirin) to relieve pain. As far back as 10,000 years ago, prehistoric healers performed **surgery.** The earliest known surgical procedure was an operation called *trephining,* in which a hole was cut in the patient's skull to relieve pressure on the brain. This procedure, discovered in prehistoric skeletal remains, is still in use today!

5.   Hippocrates, the ancient physician commonly considered the father of medicine, was born in Greece in 460 B.C. Although the Greeks of this period were still seeking medical cures at the temple of the Greek god of healing, Hippocrates maintained that disease had only natural causes. Hippocrates is credited with being the first physician to separate the art and science of medicine from the practice of religion. Though its authorship is unknown, the famous Hippocratic oath is named for him. In the Western world, it is a long-standing tradition for physicians, when they graduate from medical school, to swear to uphold the high ideals outlined in this oath. They promise (among other things) to maintain the utmost respect for human life and to respect the confidentiality of the doctor-patient relationship.

6.   Fragments of pre-Christian Egyptian writings describe a routine still followed by most doctors—moving from the patient's symptoms to physical **examination** and then to suggested **therapy** and **prognosis.**

7.   Also in the ancient world of the Middle East, the Babylonian Code of Hammurabi (dated 2040 B.C. and inscribed on a great stone pillar) contained statements about the proper conduct of physicians and prescribed punishments for malpractice.

8.   Ancient medical advances in the Far East were also significant. In India, early medical marvels included the discovery of the relationship between malaria and mosquitos, the discovery of more than 700 medicinal plants, and the invention of more than 100 surgical instruments. In the fifth century A.D., the great Indian physician Susruta was treating fractures, removing tumors, and delivering babies by Caesarean section.

9.   The medical therapy called **acupuncture**—which involves inserting needles into selective sites on the surface of the body—has been a part of Chinese medicine since ancient times. Although it was originally used to treat disease, acupuncture's effectiveness in sometimes controlling chronic pain has recently become more widely acknowledged by the Western world. How and why are not known, but some scientists believe that the needles may stimulate the brain to produce morphinelike painkilling chemicals called *endorphins* and *enkephalins.*

10.   In the second century A.D., the Greek physician Galen revolutionized medicine by his insistence upon the study of anatomy as a basis for medical facts. The only problem was that his anatomical research was done on nonhuman animals, and he sometimes mistakenly assumed greater similarity than was correct between the animals he dissected and the human body.

11.   The historical period commonly called the Middle Ages dates from about 500 A.D. to about 1500 A.D. The period from 500 A.D. to about 1000 A.D. is often referred to as the Dark Ages, meaning that there was widespread ignorance and a lack of progress in the ability of people to understand and control their environment. During the Middle Ages in Europe, Christian compassion for the sick led to the building of many hospitals and the founding of the first medical schools. However, as in ancient times, disease was considered supernatural in origin, and treatment was often a mixture of prayer and magic. Still, after the bubonic plague killed one-fourth of the European population in the mid-14th century, scientists became more determined to search for practical, effective methods of dealing with medical problems.

12.   The period called the Renaissance (which began in the 14th century in Italy and spread throughout Europe) was characterized by a great revival in learning. During this period, medical knowledge increased rapidly,

aided greatly by the development of printing. Laws forbidding the **dissection** of **cadavers** were relaxed, and as a result, the first accurate textbook on human anatomy was published, correcting Galen's errors.

13.   During the Renaissance, many traditional surgical techniques were reevaluated and revised. A French physician named Paré (generally considered the father of modern surgery) opposed the practice of burning (**cauterizing**) wounds and introduced the use of ligatures to stop bleeding.

14.   In 1545, the first pharmacy was opened in London. Prescription medicines had been administered prior to this time, but establishment of this shop indicated that medication was becoming an accepted means of treating disease. Today, many thousands of **drugs** are used to treat illness.

15.   The microscope (which greatly enlarges very small objects) was invented in 1590. This tool has since become indispensable in the **diagnosis** of disease. Laboratory technicians use it regularly to analyze **specimens** of **blood,** urine, and **tissue.** Their reports provide physicians with valuable information which could not otherwise be known.

16.   In the early 1600s, the English physician William Harvey discovered how blood circulates in the body and published the first medical book describing this circulation and the role of the heart in producing it. In 1667, the first blood **transfusion** was performed.

17.   In the 19th century, modern surgery was made possible by two revolutionary discoveries: the invention of safe methods of **anesthesia** and the control of wound infection by the use of antiseptics and sterile equipment. Also in this century, a set diagnostic procedure — requiring a complete **case history** and a thorough physical examination — became common medical practice. Finally, in 1895, came Roentgen's discovery of the **X-ray.**

18.   The 20th century has brought amazing medical advances in nearly every area of medicine. Open-heart surgery has been developed. **Organ transplants** are often successful. Vaccines (infectious agents given to patients to establish resistance to particular diseases) have virtually eliminated the threat of poliomyelitis (an infectious disease that can cause paralysis). The electrocardiogram (EKG) and electroencephalogram (EEG) help physicians detect heart and brain malfunctions, respectively. Due to earlier diagnosis and more effective treatment, more and more cancer victims are surviving. Sophisticated X-ray techniques allow more accurate diagnoses and more effective treatment. Lasers (powerful beams of light) make many surgical procedures faster and easier.

19.   Despite incredible advances in medical science, health workers know that the search for better medical care will never end. As human beings alter their lifestyles and their environment, new diseases and debilitating conditions develop to challenge medical research. There can be no conclusion to the history and advancement of medicine as long as people inhabit the earth.

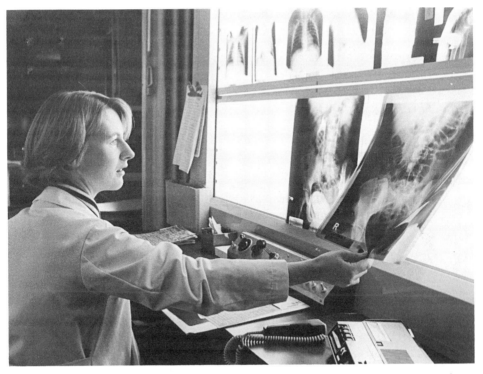

Sophisticated X-ray techniques allow doctors to provide more accurate diagnoses and more effective treatment. (*Laimute E. Druskis*)

SPECIAL TERMS

Some Steps in Medical Consultation

case history — the patient's complete medical background, including past physical and mental conditions, the medical problems of close family members, and the patient's present complaints, behavior, and lifestyle.

diagnosis — the use of scientific methods to determine the cause and nature of a patient's illness.

examination — careful study of the patient's body to determine the presence or absence of disease or abnormality. A complete physical exam usually includes inspection (looking), palpation (touching and feeling), percussion (tapping), and auscultation (listening).

prognosis — prediction of the course and end of a disease and the outlook for the patient's future health based upon this.

therapy — treatment of a disease or pathological condition.

Some Forms of Treatment

acupuncture — the insertion of needles along various nerve-root pathways of the body for diagnostic or therapeutic purposes.

cauterize — to burn or destroy dead tissue by heat, electricity, or chemicals. Cauterization is often used to stop bleeding or promote the healing of inflammation.

drug — any substance that, when taken into the body, may modify one or more of the body's functions. The word is often used as a synonym for *medicine.*

surgery — the branch of medicine dealing with operative procedures used to correct defects, repair injuries, diagnose or cure diseases, relieve pain, or prolong life.

transfusion — the intravenous (into the vein) administration of life-saving fluids such as blood or plasma.

transplant — to transfer an organ or tissue from one part of the body to another, or from one person or animal to another, in order to lessen a defect or remedy a deformity or injury.

X-ray — a high-energy electromagnetic wave used to diagnose and treat disease. Photographs obtained by this method are called X-rays.

Other Medical Vocabulary

anesthesia — insensibility to pain or touch. Drugs that cause anesthesia are anesthetics. The two major types are general (affecting the whole body) and local (affecting only a part of the body). Anesthetics can be inhaled or given by injection. Topical anesthetics are applied externally.

blood — the fluid that circulates through the heart, arteries, veins, and capillaries. A person who is losing blood is *bleeding* or *hemorrhaging.*

cadaver — a dead body, a corpse.

dissection — the cutting of parts of the body in order to study them.

heal — to cure, make whole or healthy.

organ — a part of the body having a special function. Many organs are in pairs, such as the eyes, ears, lungs, kidneys, and (in women) the ovaries.

specimen — part of a thing intended to show the nature and quality of the whole (for example, a urine specimen).

tissue — a group of similar cells that work together to perform a particular function (connective tissue, muscular tissue, etc.).

VOCABULARY PRACTICE

1. What is the difference between preventing a disease and curing or healing the patient? *diagnosis*

2. What are the four general techniques of physical examination? Name and define each. *Inspection, Palpation, Percussion auscultacion.*

3. What is the difference between a general and a local anesthetic? *Local afect. only a part of the body and general afect the whole body*

4. What two general medical uses are there for X-rays? *High energy electronic and Photographs.*

5. Are all transplants from one person's body to another?

6. Why are transplants performed?

7. Why do doctors dissect cadavers?

8. What do physicians look at with a microscope — organs or tissue?

9. When and why do doctors use an anesthetic?

10. If a patient bleeds a lot during an operation, how can the lost blood be replaced?

11. What is the difference between an examination given in class by a teacher and an examination performed by a physician?

12. What are four organs that a human being has a pair of?

13. Why do doctors sometimes cauterize tissue?

14. In what different general ways can surgery help patients?

15. What is the difference between a diagnosis and a prognosis?

EXERCISES

I. DISCUSSING MEDICAL MATTERS

1. Why is the doctor's promise to obey the Hippocratic oath important to patients?

2. Have you ever received an acupuncture treatment? If so, did it help your medical condition? If not, would you ever consider using this form of treatment? Why or why not?

3. During a routine physical exam, what parts of the body does the doctor look at, listen to, feel, and tap?

4. What diseases have been almost eliminated by vaccines? What diseases are researchers now seeking vaccines for?

5. Today, most people do not believe that illness is caused by angry gods. What are considered the major causes of illness?

II. ANALYZING WORDS AND WORD PARTS

A. Discuss the meanings of these pairs of words:

biotics / antibiotics
septic / antiseptic
patient (noun and adjective) / impatient (adjective)

B. Use a dictionary to find the meaning(s) of each word part below. Then find two medical words that begin with each.

1. di- _____

   _____   _____

2. mal- _____

   _____   _____

3. pre- _____

   _____   _____

4. pro- _____

   _____   _____

5. super- _____

_____   _____

6. trans- _____

_____   _____

C. The prefix *in-* sometimes means *not* and sometimes means *in*. What does it mean in the words *inoculate* and *injection?* _____

D. What is the difference in meaning between the words *inscribe* and *prescribe?* _____

_____

What is the meaning of the word part they share? _____

E. Write the noun for each verb below. Use a dictionary for help.

1. prescribe _____   **5.** treat _____

2. examine _____   **6.** cure _____

3. bleed _____   **7.** breathe _____

4. medicate _____   **8.** diagnose _____

Now say these noun–verb pairs aloud.

III. PRONOUNCING MEDICAL AND GENERAL WORDS

A. **Pronouncing the voiceless and the voiced *th* sounds.** The letters *th* have two different sounds in English. One is *voiced* (the vocal cords vibrate to make the sound), and the other is *voiceless*. Say the following words aloud while putting the tip of your tongue between your teeth.

voiced [ð]: breathe, though, that, either

voiceless [θ]: breath, therapy, anesthetic, ether

B. **Contrasting blends with *l* and *r*.** It is important to make a clear distinction between the letters *l* and *r;* otherwise, a serious problem in communication can develop. A patient will be glad to hear that you are going to stop her *bleeding,* but not at all happy to hear that you plan to stop her *breathing!* So practice pronouncing these words very carefully:

bleed / breathe / blood / brother

breath / bred / bled

bleeding / breathing / breeding

play / pray   grow / glow   clean / cream / scream

prognosis / plot / plant

IV. USING NEW WORDS AND PHRASES

    A.   Discuss the differences in meaning between these pairs of phrases:

        1. practicing the piano / practicing medicine

        2. prescribing medicine / studying medicine

    B.   Discuss the meaning of the expression *doctor-patient relationship.* What conditions help to make it successful? What interferes or damages it? Why is it important?

    C.   Match the words that mean the same by writing the correct numbers on the lines below.

    1. examine   _____ prediction

    2. illness   _____ vaccination

    3. inoculation   _____ doctor

    4. instruments   _____ sample

    5. physician   _____ utensils, tools

    6. procedure   _____ method, way

    7. prognosis   _____ inspect, look at

    8. specimen   _____ operation

    9. surgery   _____ live

   10. survive   _____ ailment

D. Fill in the blanks with the verbs *gives, takes, prescribes, prepares,* and *fills.*

1. The doctor _____ medicine for a patient.

2. The pharmacist _____ or

_____ the prescription.

3. The nurse _____ the medicine to the hospitalized patient.

4. The patient _____ (swallows) the medicine.

V. CHECKING COMPREHENSION

A. Put the following activities in chronological order, in the order that a physician normally does them when a new, nonemergency patient comes to the office. Number them from 1 to 6.

_____ Prescribe therapy.

_____ Take a case history.

_____ Examine the patient.

_____ Order medical tests.

_____ Make a prognosis.

_____ Make a diagnosis.

B. An *inference* is a logical, probable conclusion based upon information given. Make inferences to answer questions about the paragraphs listed below:

¶10, 12: Why didn't Galen cut up cadavers? _____

_____

¶12: What was the significance of the first dissection? _____

_____

¶7, 11: Was the year 1500 A.D. before or after 2046 B.C.? _____

CHAPTER 2

Human Anatomy

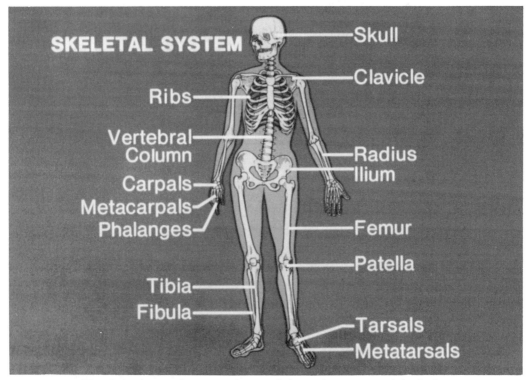

The skeletal-muscular system is one of the major systems of the body.

1.   The human body is a remarkably complex and efficient machine. It takes in and absorbs oxygen through the **respiratory system.** Then the oxygen-enriched blood is distributed through the **cardiovascular system** to all tissues. The **digestive system** converts digestible food to energy and disposes of the rest. The **skeletal-muscular** system gives form to the body. And covering almost the entire mass is the skin, the largest organ of the body. The science of the structure of this complicated "machine" is called *anatomy.*

2.   One of the major systems is the skeletal-muscular system. The body is supported and given shape by this structure, consisting of more than 200 bones and the **muscles** and **tendons** which are connected to them. They are strong but can bend at their joints. They also serve as a shield, protecting the vital internal organs from injury.

3.   Bones are as strong as steel but much lighter and more flexible. They are composed of minerals, organic matter, and water, held together by a cementlike substance called *collagen,* and are filled with red and yellow bone marrow. The red marrow produces the red blood cells used throughout the body to transport oxygen, while the yellow marrow consists primarily of fat cells. A tough membrane called the *periosteum* covers most of the bone surface and allows bones to be nourished by blood.

4.   A major bone structure in the body is the vertebral (spinal) column. It runs up and down the back and protects the spinal cord, where many of the major nerves are located. It is composed of bony vertebrae which are held together by ligaments of connective tissue and separated from each other by spinal discs. At the top of the vertebral column is the skull, which surrounds and protects the brain. Attached to the vertebral column below the neck are the 12 pairs of ribs, comprising the rib cage. At the bottom is the sacrum, which connects the vertebral column to the pelvis. Bones are united by joints and held together by ligaments.

5.   Muscles are special fibrous tissues found throughout the body. They control movement and many organic functions by contracting in response to nerve signals. Skeletal muscles are called voluntary because they can be consciously controlled. They are attached to bones by tough fibrous tissues called tendons. Other muscles, such as the stomach muscles and the heart, are involuntary and are operated automatically by the central nervous system.

6.   Healthy muscles are said to have good muscle tone. Not all muscles are healthy, however, for various ailments may affect them. An inflammation of a tendon (tendonitis), of the protective sac at a joint (bursitis), or of a muscle itself (myositis) may occur. When a muscle becomes fatigued, it sometimes contracts violently and painfully. This condition is known as *cramping.* Too much strenuous activity may produce a *strain.*

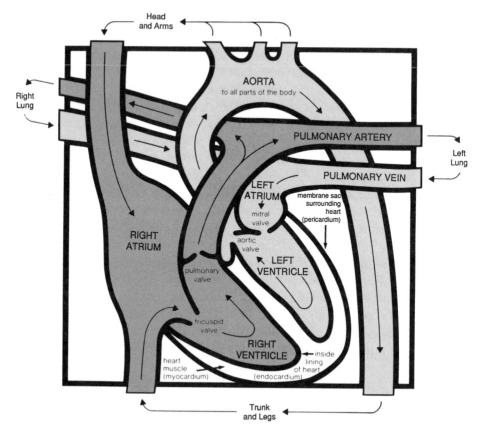

This schematic illustrates the flow of blood through the heart. (*American Heart Association*)

7.   The most important muscle in the body is the heart. Without the heart and its cardiovascular (circulatory) system, human life would not be possible. The heart is roughly the size of two fists (about 5 inches in length). It contracts at an average rate of 72 times per minute or nearly 38,000,000 times in a year. These rhythmic contractions are called the pulse rate and can be felt in the radial artery of the wrist.

8.   The human heart consists of four chambers, two **atria** (or auricles) and two **ventricles.** Each is made up of several layers of cardiac muscle arranged in circles and spirals. During the contraction phase, called the *systole,* oxygenated blood is pumped out of the left ventricle into the aorta and from there through the arteries to all organs of the body. Carbon dioxide, a waste product of this process, is collected in the blood. The blood is passed back to the right atrium through the veins and the *vena cava* during the *diastole* (or relaxation) period of the heart. From there, it is pumped into

the right ventricle and to the pulmonary artery to be sent to the lungs, where carbon dioxide is removed and oxygen is added.

9.   The rest of the system consists of arterioles (small arteries), venules (small veins), and capillaries, the smallest of **blood vessels.** In total, there are more than 70,000 miles of blood vessels in the human body!

10.   The cardiovascular system also carries hormones which are secreted by glands of the **endocrine system** directly into the bloodstream. These hormones control many functions of the body. The thyroid gland, for example, secretes thyroxin, which controls the rate at which energy is produced (the metabolic rate).

11.   The blood is made up of two parts—plasma and blood cells. The plasma is a clear, yellowish liquid which transports the 25,000,000,000,000 (25 trillion) red blood cells (erythrocytes) and the many fewer white cells (leukocytes). The red cells carry the protein hemoglobin, which carries oxygen to the body cells. The white cells are important in fighting disease. Platelets in the blood permit clotting to take place at the site of a wound, thus preventing excessive bleeding.

12.   The respiratory system starts at the nasal passages (nose), where air is breathed in during inspiration. There the air is filtered and its temperature regulated. It then passes through the larynx (voice box) and trachea (windpipe) into the bronchi and bronchioles, and ends in little air pockets called *alveoli* within the lungs. The used blood is cleansed of carbon dioxide, which is expelled in the process known as *expiration*. The cleansed blood is then oxygenated and redistributed along the circulatory system. The entire process is called *respiration* and occurs at the rate of about 16 to 20 times per minute.

13.   The largest organ in the body is the outer covering called *skin*. (The average man has about 20 square feet of it.) The skin plus its associated structures (hair, nails, sebaceous and sweat **glands,** and specialized sensory receptors that enable the body to be aware of touch, cold, heat, pain, and pressure) make up the **integumentary system.** Skin protects the body from microbes and other impurities, prevents the loss of body fluids, and regulates body temperature. Three layers of tissue make up the skin—the **epidermis,** the **dermis,** and the **subcutis** (subcutaneous layer). The epidermis is in constant growth, with its outer layer of dead cells continuously being replaced as new cells are formed in the lower layer. Hair, fingernails, and toenails are specialized forms of epidermis. The coloring pigment called *melanin* is also found in the epidermis. The middle layer (or dermis) is the location for two main types of glands—sweat glands and oil glands. The innermost subcutis contains fat cells, blood vessels, and nerves.

14.   Another major body complex is the digestive system, which processes the food so that it can be used for energy. The process begins in the

mouth, where food is chopped and crushed by the teeth. In the mouth, saliva, excreted by the salivary glands, provides enzymes that help to break down the food's carbohydrates. This taking of food into the body for digestion is called *ingestion.*

15.   After food has been chewed, it passes through the esophagus into the stomach. Peristaltic movements in the walls of the esophagus help push the food along the alimentary canal. The muscular walls of the stomach continue the mixing process while secreting hydrochloric acid from the 35,000,000 glands in the stomach lining. After 30 minutes to three hours in the stomach, the food is converted into a semiliquid state and passes into the small intestine, a tube about 20 feet long located in the lower abdomen. Here, enzymes from pancreatic fluid and bile from the liver complete the digestive process. Nutrients are absorbed into the blood through the villi, which line the walls of the digestive organs. These nutrients are either used in maintaining the body or are burned for energy. What cannot be absorbed is passed out through the large intestine as feces. Liquid wastes are eliminated through the **urinary system.** They are picked up by the blood and removed by the kidneys. From there they pass through the ureter, bladder, and urethra, and are excreted from the body as urine.

16.   Closely associated with the urinary system is the **reproductive system,** by which human life is carried on to future generations. Sperm cells are produced in the testicles of the male and ejaculated through the penis into the female vagina. The fertilization of the female's ovum (egg) by the male's sperm is called *conception.* It usually occurs in one of the fallopian tubes, which the sperm reaches through active movement from the place of deposition. Normally, the fertilized egg then travels to the uterus where it becomes an embryo, is implanted, and develops for about 280 days (until childbirth).

17.   The **nervous system** controls all other systems and bodily movements. Nerves carry sensory impulses to the central nervous system and motor impulses from the central nervous system. Motor impulses are those that control muscles. Sensory impulses affect the senses that enable human beings to feel, see, taste, and so forth.

18.   The nervous system is divided into the central nervous system (the brain and spinal cord) and the peripheral nervous system, which consists of the nerves that connect muscles and sensory organs with the central nervous system. The central nervous system is responsible for sending impulses to the voluntary muscles. The autonomic system, a part of the peripheral nervous system, regulates the involuntary muscles and organs.

19.   The brain is not only the most important component of the nervous system; it is also the controller of all bodily activities, thoughts, and emotions. It is composed of the pons, medulla oblongata, cerebellum, and

cerebrum. The cerebellum is the area of the brain that coordinates the voluntary muscles; the medulla oblongata controls the involuntary muscles; the pons is where many important nerves originate.

20.   It is the cerebrum that gives humans their ability to think, remember, and conceptualize. It is divided vertically into two halves known as the left and right hemispheres. The left hemisphere processes verbal functions, while the right hemisphere is involved in nonverbal activities and is the seat of human creativity. Many scientists believe that, in each individual, one of the two hemispheres is dominant, and that the individual has greater intellectual strength in the dominant hemisphere.

21.   It is amazing how well each system functions and coordinates with other systems to enable humans to live, reproduce, and create.

SPECIAL TERMS

General Vocabulary

human anatomy — the study of the structure and organs of the human body. It includes *gross anatomy* (structures that can be seen with the naked eye) and *microscopic anatomy* or *histology* (the study of tissues under a microscope).

system — a group of structures or organs related to each other and working together to perform certain functions.

Major Systems of the Body

cardiovascular (circulatory) system — the system that carries blood to various parts of the body. It consists of the heart, blood vessels, and lymphatic system.

digestive system — all the organs and glands involved in the ingestion and digestion of food, from the mouth to the anus.

endocrine system — the ductless glands that produce internal secretions and secrete these directly into the blood or lymph and circulate it to all body parts. These glands include the thyroid, parathyroid, adrenal cortex, adrenal medulla, anterior pituitary, posterior pituitary, testes, and ovaries.

integumentary system—the skin (the largest organ in the body) and its associated structures, including hair, nails, and sweat and sebaceous glands.

nervous system—a system of nerve cells including the brain, cranial nerves, spinal cord, spinal nerves, autonomic ganglia, and other nerves that handle the functions of reception of and response to stimuli. The nervous system regulates and coordinates bodily activities and enables the body to adjust to external and internal changes.

reproductive system—the system that enables human beings to have offspring. The male reproductive (genital) organs are mostly external and include the penis, the scrotum, and two testicles (testes) contained in the scrotum. The female sex organs are internal and include the vagina (with its opening covered by folds of skin called the *vulva*), the uterus, fallopian tubes, and ovaries.

respiratory system—the system that brings oxygen into the body and removes carbon dioxide. This process, called breathing, involves two acts: inspiration and expiration. The organs of this system are the nose, tonsils, pharynx, bronchi, pleura, and lungs.

skeletal-muscular system—the system that protects and supports the internal organs and also helps the body move. The skeleton has 206 named bones including the skull, vertebral column, ribs, and the bones of the legs, hips, and shoulders. Surrounding the bones and soft organs of the body are more than 650 muscles.

urinary system—the system that removes urea and other waste materials from the body in a liquid called *urine*. These waste materials come from the cells, go into the bloodstream, and then travel through the kidneys, ureters, bladder, urethra, and out of the body.

Chambers of the Heart

atria—the upper chambers of the heart. The left atrium receives oxygenated blood from the lungs; the right atrium receives deoxygenated blood from the rest of the body.

ventricles—the lower chambers of the heart, which, when filled with blood, contract and propel it into the arteries.

Layers of the Skin

epidermis — the protective outer layer, which contains pigment-forming cells that determine skin color.

dermis (also called *derma, corium,* and *cutis*) — the middle layer, which contains blood vessels, sweat glands, and nerves that convey sensation.

subcutis (or *subcutaneous layer*) — the layer below the dermis. It contains blood vessels, nerves, and connective tissue for padding, insulation against heat and cold, and storage of food and water.

Other Body Parts

blood vessel — a tube that carries blood. A large blood vessel that carries blood away from the heart is called an artery. Smaller vessels with the same function are arterioles. Veins and venules return blood to the heart. The two systems are united by tiny capillaries.

gland — an organized collection of tissue that can manufacture and release a secretion which is then used in some other part of the body. Exocrine glands have ducts; endocrine glands don't.

muscle — tissue composed of fibers that shorten by contraction to produce movement.

tendon — fibrous connective tissue that attaches muscles to bones and to other muscles.

VOCABULARY PRACTICE

1. What are some important functions of the skin?

2. Which layer of skin contains the sweat glands, and what do these glands do to help the human body?

3. Which tissues enable the body to move?

4. Which vessels carry blood to the heart, and which carry it away?

5. What is the difference between gross anatomy and histology?

6. What is the difference between an organ and a system? Which is the skin?

7. What does a gland do? Name three important glands in the human body, and tell their functions.

8. What is the difference between an endocrine gland and an exocrine gland?

9. What is the difference between ingestion and digestion? Where does ingestion occur? Where does digestion occur?

10. Which system controls breathing? What are its organs?

11. Which system coordinates the activities of the other systems?

12. Which system contains the genital organs?

13. What is the name of the tissue that connects muscle to bone?

14. What is another name for the circulatory system?

15. What are capillaries? Which system do they belong to?

EXERCISES

I. DISCUSSING MEDICAL MATTERS

1. What specific kinds of problems can interfere with normal breathing? Discuss some examples of foreign bodies, injuries, inflammatory conditions, allergic conditions, etc., and name some appropriate methods of treatment.

2. What are some life-threatening cardiovascular problems?

3. How is a fracture (broken bone) usually treated?

4. Name some external organs that come in pairs. Discuss the advantages of having two instead of one.

5. What are some ways that messages get to the human brain?

II. ANALYZING WORDS AND WORD PARTS

A. Many nouns relating to medical conditions do not form their plural by adding *-s* or *-es*. Instead, they have irregular plural forms, generally from Latin or Greek. Write the plural of each medical word below. Use a dictionary for help, if necessary.

1. atrium _____

2. bronchus _____

3. ganglion _____

4. pleura _____

5. stimulus _____

6. testis _____

B. After each word part below, write its meaning. Then write a word which contains that word part. Use a dictionary for help.

1. cardi- _____   _____

2. cerebr- _____   _____

3. cutane- _____   _____

4. derm- _____   _____

5. hist- _____   _____

6. leuc- _____   _____

7. para- _____   _____

8. peri- _____   _____

9. pharyng- _____   _____

10. -stalsis _____   _____

11. systol- _____   _____

12. vas- _____   _____

C. The word *anatomy* comes from a Greek word meaning *cut up*. What is the connection? _____

_____

D. The prefix *in-* sometimes means *in*. Its opposite is *ex-*, which means *out, without,* or *away.*

1. What is the difference between *internal organs* and *external organs?*

_____

_____

2. When discussing respiration, what is the difference between *inspiration* and *expiration?* What other meanings do these two words have?

_____

_____

_____

E. Many medical words also have a related nonmedical meaning.

1. What is the general meaning of the word *atrium?* _____

_____

What does it mean in relation to the heart? _____

_____

2. What is the general meaning of the word *ventricle?* _____

_____

What does it mean in relation to the heart? _____

_____

III. PRONOUNCING MEDICAL AND GENERAL WORDS

A. Read the following sentences aloud in class:

1. This candy is very sweet.

2. The sweat glands of the skin secrete sweat (perspiration).

3. My friend told me a secret.

4. The patient was hemorrhaging from the site of the wound.

5. The sight of the blood made the little boy cry.

6. I wound a bandage around the patient's wound.

B.   The letters *sc* sometimes sound like an *s* and sometimes sound like *sk*. In general, if the *c* is followed by an *e, i,* or *y,* the sound is [s], but if it is followed by any other letter, the sound is [sk]. However, there are exceptions to this general rule (for example, the word *muscle*). Pronounce these words aloud:

[s]: muscle, scissors, science, sciatica, scene

[sk]: muscular, miscarriage, scalp, scrotum, scar, scan, schizophrenia, scheme

C.   The letters *ph* make the sound [f]. Say the following words aloud:

esophagus, peripheral, diaphragm, phase, phrase

D.   In many English words, two vowels next to each other are pronounced separately. Say the following words aloud:

fluid, coordinate, create, aorta, periosteum, trachea

IV. USING NEW WORDS AND PHRASES

Match the medical words with the common words that mean the same by writing the correct numbers on the lines. Use a dictionary, if necessary. Then say the medical words aloud.

1. clavicle	_____ kneecap
2. larynx	_____ spine
3. patella	_____ shoulder blade
4. phalanges	_____ windpipe
5. scapula	_____ collarbone
6. sternum	_____ breastbone
7. trachea	_____ voice box

8. uterus   _____ womb

9. vertebral column   _____ bones of a finger or toe

V. CHECKING COMPREHENSION

A.   Select the correct answer to complete each sentence.

    1. According to paragraph 1, *disposes of* means **(a)** eliminates; **(b)** burns; **(c)** absorbs.

    2. In paragraph 3, the word *cementlike* means **(a)** strong; **(b)** soft; **(c)** made of stone.

    3. According to paragraph 11, one trillion equals **(a)** a thousand million; **(b)** a thousand billion; **(c)** a hundred billion.

B.   In the first paragraph of this chapter, the human body is compared to a machine. In what sense is this analogy true? In what ways is the body different from a machine?

C.   Mark each statement below **T** *(true)* or **F** *(false)*. Correct the statements that are false.

1. _____ Bronchi are part of the skeleton.

2. _____ The most important muscle in the body is the heart.

3. _____ Hemoglobin is a protein found in white blood cells.

4. _____ The top layer of skin is constantly dying and being replaced.

5. _____ Capillaries are secretions which help with the digestion of food.

6. _____ Oxygen is breathed into the body during inspiration, and carbon dioxide is released during expiration.

7. _____ The pulse is a measure of the heartbeat.

8. _____ The vertebral column is composed of a number of flexible dendrites.

9. _____ Liquid wastes are passed out of the body through the rectum.

10. _____ The heart contracts at an average rate of 18 times per minute.

CHAPTER 3

Disease:
Its Symptoms
and Treatments

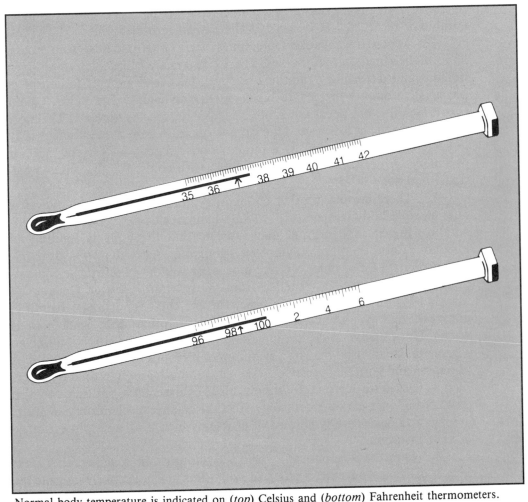

Normal body temperature is indicated on (*top*) Celsius and (*bottom*) Fahrenheit thermometers. (*Becton Dickinson and Company*)

1. Diseases and treatments can be categorized in several ways: by their cause, by the system of the body affected, by severity, by the usual form of treatment, by the likelihood of recurrence, or by the expected outcome. A physician studies the patient's medical history, **symptoms,** current physical condition, and medical test results in order to make a diagnosis and answer these kinds of questions: Is the condition serious (major) or minor? Is the patient suffering from a **chronic** problem or an **acute** attack? If there is a tumor, is it benign or malignant (cancerous)? Is it localized or widespread? If the patient has a runny nose and a postnasal drip, are these conditions caused by an **infection** or an allergy? If there is an infection, what type of germ is it caused by? Is the disease communicative (contagious) or noncontagious? Is this a physical or a mental illness, or both? What is the treatment of choice? What is the course of the illness likely to be? Is the patient's illness curable or incurable? Is it fatal? Is the patient terminally ill?

2. Tentative diagnoses sometimes begin with patients, who notice abnormal changes in their bodies. These changes are called *symptoms.* Two obvious and disturbing symptoms which usually lead patients to consult a physician promptly are severe bleeding (**hemorrhaging**) and pain. A pain that is bearable but persistent is often labeled an *ache* by patients. The most common are the headache and the stomach ache. A pain in the stomach may indicate simple indigestion or a more serious ailment such as an ulcer or dysentery. A headache may be associated with colds, the flu, sinus infections, and head injuries.

3. There are many other common symptoms of ill health. **Fever** is one. Normal body temperature is 98.6° Fahrenheit or 37° Celsius. A temperature higher than normal may indicate that the body is fighting an infection. Another common symptom is coughing. A **cough** may be dry, or it may produce a lot of phlegm (thick mucus) or sputum (a substance containing a variety of material expelled from the respiratory tract). Coughs are associated with ailments of the nose, throat, chest, and lungs. Fainting, dizziness, and persistent fatigue are other symptoms that something is wrong. One possible cause is a low red blood cell count, a condition known as **anemia,** which itself may be a symptom of a serious illness. The symptoms of **nausea** and vomiting are associated with stomach and intestinal disorders such as the flu (influenza), food poisoning, or dysentery, but they can also result from inner-ear disorders that affect the balance mechanism. Sweating, itching, and rashes are symptoms of problems such as allergies, insect bites, or skin irritations.

4. Sometimes a patient's various symptoms fit together and form what is called a **syndrome,** a group of symptoms that collectively indicate the presence of a particular disease or condition. An example of this is Reye's

syndrome, an acute, very serious childhood illness that in its first stage is characterized by abdominal pain, vomiting, severe weakness, and liver dysfunction.

5.   In order to treat an illness successfully and prevent a recurrence, a physician usually needs to identify not only the condition but also its cause. The first step is to ascertain whether the illness is infectious or noninfectious. An infectious disease is caused by microorganisms (minute living bodies that are invisible to the naked eye). These tiny organisms (bacteria, viruses, fungi, protozoa, or worms) are also called **pathogens** or, more commonly, *germs.* Infectious diseases are often (but not always) communicable (contagious), which means that an infected person can pass the disease to another through direct or indirect contact. Diseases not caused by pathogens are classified as *noninfectious.* In this category are chronic degenerative diseases characterized by the breakdown of tissues and/or organs (often the result of aging), congenital defects (those existing from birth), hormonal disorders, environmental and occupational diseases, immunological diseases, and mental illness. One cause of illness that doctors dislike even thinking about is the iatrogenic disorder (an abnormal condition caused by the physician's treatment). Finally, there are disease conditions labeled *idiopathic*—which means without any recognizable causes.

6.   Whether a person exposed to pathogens becomes ill or not depends upon the body's ability to resist microorganisms. This ability is termed **immunity** and may be natural or acquired. Natural immunity is provided by such bodily defense mechanisms as (a) the skin, tears, and the mucous membranes that line the mouth, nose, and bronchial tubes; (b) harmless bacteria in the body which interfere with the growth of harmful germs;

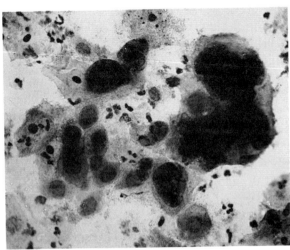

The herpes simplex virus. (*National Institutes of Health*)

(c) stomach juices that are highly acidic and also contain disease-fighting chemicals; and (d) specialized white blood cells that live in the tissues, fluids, and blood.

7.   Acquired immunity is developed by exposure to germs and their products and depends on specific **antibodies** produced by sensitized plasma cells. Introducing germs into the body artificially in a controlled manner stimulates the body to produce the antibodies that will prevent the growth of the same antigen in the future. **Vaccines** are used to produce an acquired immunity. A person is vaccinated with a living but weakened germ, a killed germ, or a toxic poison from the germ. Because this acquired immunity often does not last a lifetime, it may be necessary to immunize people periodically with booster shots of the vaccine.

8.   Whether a person's illness is infectious or noninfectious, there is always the hope that the doctor and the pharmacist will have a "magic potion" which, once swallowed, will make all signs and symptoms of disease disappear forever. Substances prescribed or recommended to treat illness are called *drugs* or *medicine.* In past centuries, people often found effective drugs through a process of trial and error. Today, medical personnel have a clear idea of how and why a particular drug works and what its side effects and **contraindications** are. *The Physician's Desk Reference* lists and describes various drugs on the market in the United States and shows illustrations of them. About 2,000 different drugs are currently available for the treatment of illness, and new ones are continually being developed.

9.   Many drugs are available by **prescription** only. These drugs are potent and may be dangerous if taken in an **overdose.** Some are **addictive;** therefore, their use must be strictly controlled. A patient can buy these medicines only if a doctor writes a prescription (or order) for a pharmacist to fill.

10.   Antibiotic drugs are often called "miracle drugs" because of their ability to bring rapid improvement and quick cures of some serious infections. Penicillin, a well-known antibiotic, is generally effective against a variety of bacterial infections. Made from fungi, penicillin inhibits the growth of disease-producing microorganisms. The *mycin* drugs, such as streptomycin, often work where penicillin fails or when a patient is allergic to penicillin.

11.   **Narcotic** drugs such as codeine and morphine can also be obtained only with a prescription. They are addictive and thus can be used only in restricted dosages. Originally derived from opium and now mostly synthetic, they are excellent painkillers, but in excessive amounts they can cause coma or death.

12.   Other familiar drugs include digitalis (which helps strengthen the failing heart), anticoagulants (which prevent blood clots), and diuretics

(which help remove excess fluid from the body). Insulin is used in the treatment of diabetes.

13.   Many other drugs that do not require a doctor's prescription are available in pharmacies (drugstores). One of the most well-known and widely used is aspirin. Aspirin has long been taken to relieve pain and reduce inflammation and fever. However, in recent years, a valuable new use for it has been discovered. Many patients with heart conditions take aspirin on a daily basis because its blood-thinning properties lower the risk of heart attack.

14.   Although there is no drug to **cure** the upper respiratory viral infection called the common cold, many drugs help to relieve the symptoms. Aspirin is an effective painkiller and anti-inflammatory drug, but it is contraindicated for colds or flu because it has been suspected of being a contributory cause of Reye's syndrome. To relieve the aches that accompany a cold or the flu, physicians generally prescribe acetaminophen (commonly known by the brand name *Tylenol*), especially for children. A decongestant may decrease nasal stuffiness and relieve a runny nose. Gargling with salt water or sucking on lozenges or hard candy can soothe a sore throat.

15.   Many other over-the-counter medications are used (and often overused) by the general public, including laxatives (to relieve constipation), tranquilizers, sedatives, sleeping pills, and pep pills (stimulants). Over-the-counter (nonprescription) drugs enable people to handle minor medical problems without spending money or time consulting a doctor. However, many people waste money on drugs that do not help their specific condition or that may even do more harm than good.

16.   Of course, medication is just one of many ways to treat illness. Among the other tools which physicians use are surgery, radiation therapy, chemotherapy, special equipment prescribed for patient use, and nonmedical recommendations for a change in a patient's lifestyle (following special diets, increasing or altering habits of exercise, moving to a different climate, decreasing workload and stress, and so on).

17.   As medical science becomes more and more sophisticated, people live longer and develop more chronic and debilitating conditions that require medical treatment. In highly industrialized societies, pollution has created an increase in allergic and other conditions that require medical care. The challenge of modern medicine is to meet the changing medical needs of rapidly changing societies in which people have very high (sometimes unreasonably high) expectations of their doctors' curative powers. People want to live long lives and to feel as good at 80 as they felt at 20. Doctors are not magicians, but research continues with the hope that someday, whatever people's ages, they will never feel "over the hill."

SPECIAL TERMS

Some Bodily Responses to Disease or Injury

anemia — insufficiency of red blood cells.

cough — air expelled from the lungs suddenly and noisily. A cough is usually associated with a cold or a lung disease, and it may produce mucus, phlegm, or pus.

fever — an abnormally high body temperature.

hemorrhage — excessive bleeding, internally or externally.

nausea — feeling the need to vomit. It may be caused by a virus affecting the digestive system, by an inner-ear disorder, by pregnancy, or by many other conditions.

symptom — an unusual or abnormal bodily condition such as a rash, cough, fever, or pain. Often a distinction is made between *subjective* symptoms described by the patient and *objective* signs found by medical personnel and/or tests.

syndrome — a combination of symptoms usually found in a particular disease. Syndromes aid physicians in making diagnoses.

Foreign Material and the Body's Response

antibody — a protective protein that is produced in response to foreign material (an antigen, such as bacteria). Antibodies try to kill or expel the antigen from the body.

immunity — The body fights an infection with antibodies and white blood cells. This is called an *immune response.*

infection — invasion of the body by disease-producing microorganisms.

pathogen (germ) — disease-causing microorganism. Bacteria and viruses are two kinds of pathogens.

vaccine — preparation of living, weakened, or killed microorganisms injected into the body so that the body will produce antibodies to fight the infection caused by those microorganisms.

Vocabulary about Medications

addictive — causing a bodily craving for a substance (such as a drug) which results from prior usage of the substance.

contraindication — a symptom or condition indicating that a certain drug or procedure ordinarily advisable should not be used in this particular situation or by a particular patient.

dose and **overdose** — A dose is a specified quantity of a drug recommended for a patient. An overdose is an amount in excess of that quantity.

narcotic — a drug (such as morphine or codeine) that depresses the central nervous system, thereby dulling the senses, relieving pain, and sometimes inducing sleep.

prescription — a written instruction by a physician to permit a pharmacist to dispense medication to a patient.

Other Medical Vocabulary

acute — describes an ailment that comes on suddenly, has severe symptoms, and is of short duration (in contrast to a *chronic* condition).

chronic — describes an ailment that is likely to persist or recur in the patient over a considerable length of time.

cure — restore health through medical treatment.

VOCABULARY PRACTICE

1. What is the difference between a symptom and a syndrome? Between a symptom and a sign?

2. Fever, coughs, and anemia are signs of disease. Define each.

3. Temperature is measured by a thermometer graded in either Fahrenheit or Celsius degrees. What is normal body temperature on each scale?

4. What diseases is a cough usually associated with?

5. What may cause nausea?

6. What is a vaccine? What does it do?

7. What is the relationship between the words *antibody* and *antibiotic?*

8. What is an instruction written by a physician for a pharmacist called?

9. What is the difference between a prescription and a nonprescription (over-the-counter) drug?

10. What drugs stop the growth of bacteria? Give an example.

11. Why is an overdose of a narcotic dangerous to the patient?

12. Why would a physician ever prescribe an addictive drug?

13. What do germs do? Name two general types of germs.

14. What causes the human body to become immune to a particular disease?

15. What are three differences between acute and chronic conditions?

EXERCISES

I. DISCUSSING MEDICAL MATTERS

1. What was your first childhood illness that you remember? What were its symptoms? What was the treatment?

2. Do you have any allergies? If so, what are you allergic to? What types of drugs do you take for your allergy?

3. What vaccinations have you received? Have you had booster shots for any of the illnesses that you were vaccinated for?

4. When you get a bad cold, what nonprescription drugs do you use to treat the symptoms? What nonmedical forms of treatment do you commonly try to help yourself feel better?

5. Name a drug that you are familiar with, and discuss some contraindications and side effects that might prohibit its use by some patients.

II. ANALYZING WORDS AND WORD PARTS

Studying medical word parts.   In a general or a medical dictionary, look up the meaning(s) of the word parts listed below. Write the definition(s) on the line beside each word.

1. ab- _____

2. anti- _____

3. bio- _____

4. contra- _____

5. dys- _____

6. gen- _____

7. -iatric _____

8. idio- _____

9. im- _____

10. myc- _____

11. path- _____

12. sym-; syn- _____

Now find two medical words that contain each word part, and write them in your notebook.

III. PRONOUNCING MEDICAL AND GENERAL WORDS

A.   The letters *ch* have three different sounds in English. The most common sound is [tʃ], the beginning sound in *cheese*. The next most common is the sound [k], as in *architect*. Another sound is [ʃ], as in *shoe*. Say the following words aloud.

ache [ek]   chilly [tʃɪl′i]

chemistry [kɛm′ɪstri]   machine [məʃin′]

chronic [krɑn′ɪk]   technique [tɛknik′]

B.   As you learned in Chapter 2, the letters *ph* make the sound [f]. Say the following words aloud:

pharmacy   physical   physician   pharmacist

C.   The letters *gh* are often silent. When they are pronounced, they make the sound [f]. Say the following words aloud:

thought   though   through   cough   enough   rough

D.   When the last two letters of a word are -*gn* or -*gm,* the *g* is silent. When the *g* is followed by an *m* or *n* that begins a new syllable, then the *g* is pronounced. Say the following words aloud:

sign   assign   benign   phlegm   signature   malignant

E.   Read the following sentences aloud:

1. There are 60 seconds in a *minute* and 60 *minutes* in an hour.

2. Bacteria and viruses are *minute* living bodies.

Which word *minute* rhymes with *in it,* the one in sentence 1 or sentence 2? _____

IV. USING NEW WORDS AND PHRASES

A.   Match the opposites by writing the numbers on the lines.

1. acute   _____ not contagious

2. benign   _____ minor

3. communicable   _____ fever

4. major   _____ mental

5. normal body temperature   _____ chronic

6. physical   _____ malignant

7. susceptible   _____ resistant

B. Discuss the meanings of the following:

booster shot   course of an illness

runny nose   postnasal drip

over the hill   trial and error

C. After each type of drug listed below, write a disease or condition that it is used to treat. Pronounce the names of the drugs in class.

1. anticoagulant _____

2. antiseptic _____

3. aspirin _____

4. codeine _____

5. decongestant _____

6. digitalis _____

7. diuretic _____

8. insulin _____

9. laxative _____

10. penicillin _____

D. Complete the following dialogue by using some of the 20 special terms defined in this chapter. Then read the dialogue aloud.

DR. HANSON: Good morning, Janet. What brings you in to see me today?

JANET: I don't know what's wrong, but I sure have a lot of _____s. My head hurts, I have a pain in my ear, and I'm very tired.

DR. HANSON: Did you take your temperature? Do you have a _____ ?

JANET: My temperature is normal. But I still think I have some sort of _____ .

DR. HANSON: Well, since you have a _____ sinus condition, I wouldn't be surprised. Let me have a look at you. (*After the physical exam*) Janet, you have a sinus infection and a middle-ear infection. I'm going to give you a

_____ for some antibiotics.

JANET: Can you give me something for the pain, too?

DR. HANSON: Well, I try to avoid prescribing _____ drugs. Just take some extra-strength Tylenol or aspirin. That should be strong enough to keep you comfortable until the antibiotics give you some relief.

JANET: Thank you, doctor. You're a nice person, but I do hope I won't have to see you again for a while.

DR. HANSON: No such luck, Janet. I want to see you again in ten days to be

sure that we've managed to _____ you.

V. CHECKING COMPREHENSION

A. Put an *X* through the words that don't belong in the groups below.

1. *a drug*
penicillin   parasite   aspirin   digitalis   dysentery

2. *a disease*
nausea   anemia   cancer   virus   strep throat

3. *a medical treatment*
nausea   medication   surgery   syndrome   drug

4. *pathogens*
bacteria   viruses   narcotics   parasites   fungi

5. *information used to make a diagnosis*
symptoms   medical history   treatment   prescription

6. *a symptom*
anemia   fever   cough   cure   immunity

B. Reread the paragraphs whose numbers are given in brackets. Then underline the correct word or phrase to complete each sentence.

1. [¶1] The expression *treatment of choice* means **(a)** the patient's choice; **(b)** the doctor's choice.

2. **[¶2]** A *tentative diagnosis* is made **(a)** after all relevant medical facts are known; **(b)** before all the relevant facts are known.

3. **[¶7]** If you have had *German measles,* then you won't get the disease again because you have **(a)** an acquired immunity to it; **(b)** a natural immunity to it.

4. **[¶9]** In sentence 2, the word *potent* means **(a)** ineffective; **(b)** very strong.

5. **[¶14]** *Gargling with salt water* and *sucking on lozenges* can **(a)** cure the common cold; **(b)** relieve discomfort caused by some of the symptoms.

CHAPTER 4

Common Diseases and Ailments

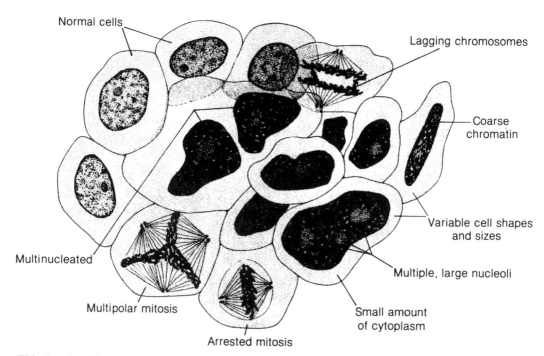

Normal cells

Lagging chromosomes

Coarse chromatin

Variable cell shapes and sizes

Multiple, large nucleoli

Multinucleated

Multipolar mitosis

Small amount of cytoplasm

Arrested mitosis

This drawing illustrates the differences between normal and cancer cells. (*Courtesy of the National Cancer Institute*)

1. There is no end in sight in the battle between human beings and the diseases that can destroy them. However, in the 20th century, the nature of the enemy has changed dramatically. In countries where modern medical facilities are available, infectious diseases that were once widespread killers can now be prevented or diagnosed early and cured. Thanks to vaccines, **antibiotics,** and improved sanitation, most of the dreaded epidemics of the past are not likely to recur.

2. Today's major killers are noninfectious diseases — especially the various forms of cardiovascular disease and cancer. As life expectancy increases, people are more likely to succumb to degenerative conditions that the aging body is susceptible to. In addition, many factors of modern life — such as environmental pollution, occupational hazards, stress, a sedentary lifestyle, an unhealthy diet, the use of cigarettes, drug and alcohol abuse — contribute to the development of disease.

3. One of the most common serious afflictions in modern society is heart disease. This general label encompasses many different abnormal conditions, including congenital heart defects (many of which can be repaired surgically), diseases of the pericardium (the tissue surrounding the heart muscle), and diseases affecting the heart muscle itself (the myocardium). Physicians can often detect or predict heart problems by measuring the rate of the heartbeat (called the **pulse**) and by taking the patient's blood pressure. Another important diagnostic tool is the electrocardiogram (EKG), a record of the electrical activity of the heart, which can reveal abnormal cardiac rhythm and myocardial damage. When heart disease is suspected and more detailed information is needed, an **angiogram** is ordered. This series of X-ray films (taken after the injection of a radiopaque substance) defines the size and shape of various veins and arteries.

4. The most common cardiovascular disease is **atherosclerosis** (hardening of the arteries). Atherosclerosis of the coronary arteries may cause the development of a coronary thrombus (blood clot), which blocks the flow of blood to the heart muscle. If, as a result, part of the heart muscle dies, the condition is called *myocardial* **infarction** (a heart attack). Some symptoms and signs of a heart attack are pain in the chest (and sometimes also in the jaws and arms), shortness of breath, irregular pulse, nausea, and perspiration. Prompt cardiopulmonary resuscitation can save victims from sudden death. Among the emergency procedures used is a technique known as *percutaneous transluminal* **angioplasty** (PTA). This technique widens coronary arteries that have become dangerously narrow due to deposits (called *plaque*) on their interior walls. The procedure involves manipulating a catheter (flexible tube) into the constricted vessel, then inflating a small balloon at its tip, thereby compressing the plaque and widening the passage.

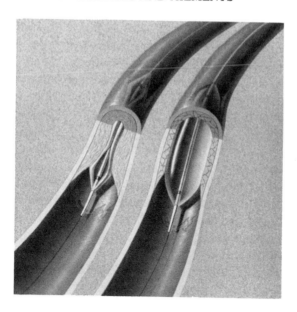

The angioplasty procedure: a balloon-tipped catheter is inserted into a plaque-filled artery (*left*); then the balloon is inflated, compressing the plaque and widening the passage (*right*). (*Courtesy of the National Heart, Lung and Blood Institute, National Institutes of Health, Department of Health and Human Services, U.S. Public Health Service*)

This procedure can sometimes substitute for a much more traumatic one—bypass surgery.

5.   When atherosclerosis affects the carotid and vertebral arteries (which supply blood to the brain), a stroke may result, causing **paralysis (paralytic stroke)** and sometimes affecting speech and brain function. Atherosclerosis can also weaken the aorta wall, causing it to develop a balloonlike structure called an **aneurysm.** Large aneurysms can rupture, causing **fatal** hemorrhage. Patients can decrease the likelihood of developing atherosclerosis by cutting down on their consumption of fats, cutting out cigarettes, and getting adequate exercise.

6.   Less serious but still frightening is the condition called **angina pectoris,** chest pains that occur when the heart muscle does not get enough oxygen (often because of a temporary spasm of a vessel). An attack is usually caused by overexertion and can be relieved by rest and nitroglycerin tablets.

7.   Patients with various kinds of heart conditions may be treated medically with many different drugs including **anticoagulants** to reduce the chance of blood clotting, beta blockers to reduce high blood pressure, or **digitalis** to increase the force of the heart's contractions. Surgical treatments include repair or replacement of valves or arteries, insertion of a pacemaker to regulate heartbeat, or even the substitution of an artificial or a transplanted human heart for the patient's diseased one.

8.   The relationship between cardiovascular disease and **hypertension** (high blood pressure) is well known, so patients with high blood pressure are

generally placed on a regimen including a low-salt diet, regular exercise, and sometimes medication that will bring the blood pressure down to within normal limits.

9.   Another major killer is cancer. Cancer is characterized by an unrestrained growth of abnormal cells. There are three main types of cancer: a *carcinoma* originates from the surface cells of the skin or the linings of the internal organs; a *sarcoma* attacks the muscles, bones, tendons, cartilage, fat, blood vessels, lymph system, or connective tissue; *leukemias* afflict the blood-forming cells. Some cancers grow slowly; others spread rapidly, doubling in bulk in days. Cancer can appear anywhere in the body, but some common sites are the lungs, breasts, uterus, skin, colon, prostate, and blood. Symptoms vary greatly depending upon the location, but some of the most common symptoms are unusual bleeding or discharge, a thickening in any area, a sore that doesn't heal, hoarseness or difficulty swallowing, indigestion, a change in bowel or bladder habits, or unexplained weight loss.

10.   Today, many types of cancer can be cured, especially if detected early. For this reason, many diagnostic procedures — such as a biopsy, mammogram, or colonoscopy (examination of the large intestine) or other internal examinations — are employed when cancer is suspected. A localized malignancy is sometimes treated and cured by surgery alone, but sometimes radiation or chemotherapy (drug or chemical treatment) is used in combination with surgery. A malignancy that has metastasized (spread from its place of origin to another organ or site) requires higher doses of chemotherapy and/or radiation and is more difficult to cure.

11.   The **etiology** of many types of cancer remains an enigma to scientists. Some of the causes are known, however, including cigarette smoking, overexposure to X-rays or sunlight, and contact with certain chemicals. Some forms of cancer seem to run in families; others may be caused by a virus.

12.   The neuromuscular systems in the body can be affected by a number of diseases. These diseases all cause a loss of muscular control by disturbing the nerves which control the muscles. In muscular dystrophy, a chronic and inherited disease, the muscles gradually **atrophy** (waste away). A patient with Parkinson's disease often exhibits uncontrollable shaking caused by basal ganglion dysfunctions. Multiple sclerosis victims suffer from a loss of muscular coordination in various parts of their bodies because of damage to nerve fibers. Unfortunately, none of these diseases is curable at present. All that can be done for a victim is to lessen the undesirable symptoms.

13.   A disease that attacks the kidneys is nephritis. There are many different types and many causes of nephritis, including bacteria and toxins. The kidneys regulate the elimination of urine from the body. If the disease

becomes severe enough to destroy the kidneys, the victim can be saved through the transplantation of a donor's kidney or by regular use of a renal **hemodialysis** machine. This machine substitutes for the kidneys, cleansing the body of its liquid wastes.

14.   Diabetes mellitus is a disease in which the body no longer uses sugar properly. In a healthy body, special cells in the pancreas secrete the hormones **insulin** and glycogen, which help to store sugar. In the body of a diabetic, these hormones are inadequately produced or utilized. The disease is usually diagnosed by the discovery of sugar in the urine and abnormally high levels of sugar in the blood. If the disease is not controlled, serious complications can develop affecting the eyes, kidneys, and circulatory system. Treatment is usually a combination of a carefully regulated diet, regular exercise, and sometimes insulin injections.

15.   Arthritis and rheumatism are general names for approximately 100 diseases that produce inflammation or degeneration of connective tissue. Some of these diseases are infectious and primarily affect younger people. Rheumatic fever, for example, is a bacterial infection that occurs mostly in children or teenagers. Rheumatoid arthritis predominantly strikes women between 20 and 60. However, the most common rheumatic disease is a noninfectious, noninflammatory degenerative joint disease—osteoarthritis. To some degree, it affects nearly all older adults, causing swelling, pain, and stiffness in joints. Treatment may include heat, exercises, and drugs that reduce pain and inflammation.

16.   Besides osteoarthritis, many other noninfectious diseases can limit the activities of the elderly. Osteoporosis (a condition in which bone loss exceeds bone replacement so that the bones become less dense, more porous, and more brittle) often leads to fractures, especially of the hip bone. Many conditions conspire to decrease the sensory perception of the elderly. Cataracts (created when the lens of the eye—or a portion of it—becomes opaque and sometimes swells or shrinks) interfere with vision. Deterioration of nerves in the inner ear causes the characteristic old-age hearing loss, most severe in the high-pitched tones. The senses of taste and smell also deteriorate in old age.

17.   But what many elderly people fear most is the loss of mental abilities. Confusion, memory loss, and inability to distinguish between reality and fantasy (dementia) are all symptoms that can be caused by damage to the brain. They may result from external injury, a stroke, or deterioration of brain cells due to inadequate blood and oxygen supply. One common cause of severe mental deterioration is Alzheimer's disease, a neurological brain disorder in which there are a variety of abnormal chemical changes in the brain and characteristic nerve cell "tangles." In the United States, about 2.5 million people are afflicted with this condition, almost 6 percent of the population over age 65 and about 20 percent of those over 85.

18.   People of all ages suffer from a variety of allergic conditions. An **allergy** is an altered reaction of body tissues to a substance which produces no effect upon a nonsensitive person. The substance causing the allergic reaction is called an *antigen*. The antibody reaction (often the release of histamine) generally makes the person feel sick or uncomfortable. Some people have food allergies (commonly to eggs, strawberries, chocolate, or nuts), and these are likely to cause skin rashes. Others are allergic to airborne particles (inhalants such as dust or pollen). These affect the respiratory tract and cause conditions such as asthma, hay fever, or allergic rhinitis. Another source of allergies is contactants (for example, wool or chemicals that come in contact with the skin). Allergies to specific drugs (penicillin, for example) are also common. Sometimes allergic reactions can be severe and lead to medical emergencies, especially if they interfere with breathing. However, most can be controlled with medication (often **antihistamines**). Of course, the best way to control an allergic condition is to avoid contact with the antigen, if possible.

19.   Among contagious diseases, many of the major killers of the past are no longer widespread problems. Smallpox, for example, has been eradicated in most parts of the world by vigorous immunization campaigns. Poliomyelitis (a disease caused by a virus which attacks the motor neurons of the spinal cord) once left large numbers of its victims temporarily or permanently paralyzed, but today vaccines effectively protect against polio. Tuberculosis, a bacterial infection which commonly affects the lungs, was the number-one killer of Americans prior to 1909. Today, to test for TB, a simple skin test is widely given periodically as part of a routine medical checkup. If the results are positive, a chest X-ray is taken to determine whether the disease is dormant or active. In either case, the condition can then be controlled or cured by medication. Another infection of the lungs, pneumonia, is also much less dangerous than it once was, thanks to antibiotics. (However, among the elderly and those weakened by other serious diseases, pneumonia is still a common cause of death.)

20.   Diseases that are common in childhood include chickenpox, measles, mumps, diphtheria, and whooping cough. In the United States, children are routinely immunized against most of these, as well as against tetanus. This is not true in all parts of the world, however, and many children suffer needlessly as a result. Fortunately, these diseases are not usually fatal.

21.   Many diseases are transmitted by sexual contact. Once called *venereal diseases,* today they are commonly called *sexually transmitted diseases* (STD). These include gonorrhea, syphilis, genital herpes, candidiasis (a yeast infection), trichomoniasis, and others. Some of these can be very destructive to the body if not treated, but all can be either cured or controlled by medication. By far the most frightening of the sexually trans-

mitted diseases is Acquired Immune Deficiency Syndrome (AIDS). This fatal disease is spread by direct sexual contact or exchange of blood (for example, by use of a contaminated hypodermic needle). AIDS destroys its victim's immune system, leaving the patient unprotected against infections that healthy people could fight off. The various "opportunistic infections" common among AIDS patients include a rare type of pneumonia and an unusual form of cancer called *Kaposi's sarcoma*. "An ounce of prevention is worth a pound of cure" is an expression that especially applies to AIDS, not only because the use of condoms and sterile needles can protect people from the disease, but also because at present there *is* no cure. Since a person can be a carrier of the HIV (human immunodeficiency virus) long before symptoms appear, people at risk are urged to take a blood test for diagnosis.

22.   At the other end of the disease spectrum are the many conditions that may make people feel temporarily "under the weather" but are not serious enough to require a physician's care—especially if they are only occasional and short-lived. Common infectious conditions such as a cold, the flu, or diarrhea (loose bowel movements) are often self-limiting and can be treated symptomatically with over-the-counter drugs. The same is true of occasional tension headaches and the monthly cramps and lower back pain that are now called *premenstrual syndrome* (PMS). People often endure the acne of adolescence and the hemorrhoids of pregnancy without consulting a physician, especially when the conditions are not severe. Minor traumas are often self-treated with routine first aid. Most people know that superficial lacerations (cuts) should be thoroughly cleaned and bandaged and that immediate immersion in cold water will relieve the pain of a slightly burned finger or a sprained ankle.

23.   The study of diseases should not make students feel fragile and vulnerable. It is important to remember that the human body has a remarkable ability to protect itself against disease and to cure itself when illness or injury does occur. Moreover, when serious illness strikes, modern medicine has extremely sophisticated tools for fighting back.

SPECIAL TERMS

Some Abnormal Conditions

allergy—an abnormal sensitivity to a particular substance so that contact with it produces an antigen-antibody reaction. For example, ragweed makes the person allergic to it sneeze.

aneurysm (*alternate spelling:* **aneurism**) — a localized abnormal dilation of a blood vessel due to a congenital defect or a weakness in the vessel wall.

angina pectoris — pain in the mid-chest that sometimes radiates to the shoulder, left arm, jaw, or abdomen. Usually brought on by physical exertion, the underlying cause is the narrowing of a blood vessel due to temporary spasm or build-up of plaque. The narrowing causes the heart to receive less blood (and therefore less oxygen) than it needs.

atherosclerosis — a form of arteriosclerosis in which there are localized accumulations of fatty material on the inside walls of blood vessels. Arteriosclerosis, a more general term, includes this condition and other degenerative blood vessel conditions such as loss of elasticity and hardening. Both conditions are commonly called hardening of the arteries.

atrophy — a wasting away due to lack of nutrition or use; also, a reduction in size of a structure after it has come to full functional maturity. Atrophy is sometimes due to an abnormal condition. For example, the calf muscles may shrink when a patient is not ambulatory for several months. However, atrophy can also be normal, as in the shrinking of the ovaries during menopause.

hypertension — abnormally high blood pressure. (Blood pressure is the pressure exerted by the blood on the wall of any vessel. What is considered normal varies somewhat with age and sex, but it is abnormally high when above 140/90.)

infarction — the death of tissue in an organ following the cessation of blood supply. Myocardial infarction (death of part of the heart muscle) usually results from a thrombus (clot) in the coronary arterial system. Coronary thrombosis may also cause cardiac arrest (a sudden cessation of heartbeat).

paralysis — temporary or permanent loss of function, especially sensation or voluntary motion.

paralytic stroke — sudden onset of paralysis caused by an injury to the brain or spinal cord.

Some Common Medications

antibiotics — a variety of substances (some natural and some synthetic) that inhibit the growth of or destroy microorganisms. They are used extensively to treat infectious diseases.

anticoagulant – an agent that prevents or delays blood coagulation. It is sometimes used following heart attacks to prevent further blood clotting or embolisms.

antihistamine – a medicine that counteracts the effect of histamine (a substance normally present in the body and in certain foods), which sometimes causes an allergic reaction. Antihistamines relieve the allergic symptoms.

digitalis – a heart stimulant drug that increases the force of the muscular contractions of the heart. It is often prescribed for patients with heart failure (a condition which means that the heart cannot maintain adequate circulation of the blood).

insulin – a hormone secreted by the pancreas; a preparation (usually prepared from the pancreas of animals) taken by hypodermic injection by some diabetic patients. Also, some patients take an oral antidiabetic drug which stimulates their pancreas to release insulin.

Other Medical Vocabulary

angiogram – an X-ray film of a blood vessel.

angioplasty – a technique for expanding a narrowed artery by inserting a balloon catheter.

etiology – the cause or causes of a disease.

fatal – resulting in death.

hemodialysis – a treatment used to cleanse the blood of patients whose kidneys are defective or absent. To remove toxic chemicals, the blood is passed through tubes made of semipermeable membranes.

pulse – rhythmic throbbing (pulsation, beating) caused by the contraction and expansion of an artery. It keeps time with the heartbeat. Normal pulse rate can range from 60 to 90 times per minute. (Athletes usually have a lower than average rate.) The pulse is usually taken by feeling the radial artery of the wrist.

VOCABULARY PRACTICE

1. What are two possible causes of an aneurysm?

2. What causes a stroke, and what may be the result?

3. If a patient has a broken arm in a cast for several weeks and cannot use the arm, what may happen to the muscles?

4. What does the prefix *anti-* mean? Name three drugs that begin with this prefix, and tell their uses.

5. Is an angiogram used for diagnosis or treatment?

6. Is angioplasty a surgical or a medical procedure?

7. What does a person's pulse rate indicate?

8. What medication is often used to treat diabetes?

9. What is the etiology of the common cold?

10. How can a person survive without functioning kidneys?

11. What do medical personnel call the death of human tissue due to insufficient blood supply?

12. Is arteriosclerosis one type of atherosclerosis or vice versa?

13. What does an anticoagulant do? Is it used to treat cancer or cardiovascular conditions?

14. What happens to the victim of a fatal disease?

15. What is the medical term for the condition commonly called *high blood pressure*?

EXERCISES

I. DISCUSSING MEDICAL MATTERS

1. What are the main reasons why noninfectious diseases have become the major killers in modern societies?

2. What are some different types of heart disease, and how are they treated?

3. What are some of the common sites of cancer in men? in women?

4. What are some common allergies, and how are they treated? Discuss an allergic condition that you are familiar with. How is it controlled?

5. Tell about a common disease not discussed in this chapter that you have had some experience with professionally or personally. Discuss etiology, symptoms, signs, treatment, and prognosis.

II. ANALYZING WORDS AND WORD PARTS

A. Write a definition of each word part below. Use a dictionary for help.

1. angio- _____

2. athero- _____

3. carcin- _____

4. dia- _____

5. -gram _____

6. -graph _____

7. -graphy _____

8. hyper- _____

9. hypo- _____

10. -itis _____

11. -osis _____

12. -plasty _____

13. -rrhea _____

14. scler- _____

15. thromb- _____

16. -trophy _____

B. Note that the prefixes *hyper-* and *hypo-* are opposites. In a general or a medical dictionary, find four medical words that begin with each prefix, and write them in your notebook.

III. PRONOUNCING MEDICAL AND GENERAL WORDS

A. Nouns and Adjectives.

1. Pronounce the noun and adjective forms of these words. Note the change in stress:

Nouns	*Adjectives*
al′lergy	aller′gic
symp′tom	symptomat′ic
trau′ma	trauma′tic

2. Pronounce the nouns and adjectives below. Notice the changes in the underlined vowel sounds.

    diab<u>e</u>tes [i]   diab<u>e</u>tic [ɛ]

    diagn<u>o</u>se [o]   diagn<u>o</u>stic [ɑ]

3. The following pair contains both stress and vowel changes:

    degeneration [didʒɛnɚe′ʃən]   degenerative [didʒɛn′ɚə tɪv]

B. Pronounce these words after your teacher. Note which syllable is stressed.

angina [ændʒɑɪ′nə]   leukemia [luki′miə]

aneurysm [æn′yɚɪzm]   osteoporosis [ɑstiopəro′sɪs]

atherosclerosis [ɑθɪrosklɛro′sɪs]   syphilis [sɪf′ɪlɪs]

dementia [dɛmɛn′ʃə]   tuberculosis [təbɚkyulo′sɪs]

IV. USING NEW WORDS AND PHRASES

A. Match each medical word or phrase with the common word or phrase that means the same.

1. anticoagulant   _____ cut

2. arrest   _____ tube

3. cardiac infarction   _____ clot

4. catheter   _____ loose stools (bowel movements)

5. diarrhea   _____ heart attack

6. etiology   _____ blood thinner

7. hypertension   _____ stoppage

8. laceration   _____ high blood pressure

9. thrombus   _____ cause; origin

B.   Complete each sentence below by underlining the correct word to complete the idea.

1. A tuberculin skin test is used for _____ .

diagnosis   treatment   vaccination   cure

2. One abnormal condition which is not common among elderly patients is _____ .

cataracts   acne   atherosclerosis   hypertension

3. A disease that may be fatal if not detected and treated early is

_____ .

arthritis   acne   cancer   headache

4. A disease that affects the neuromuscular system is _____ .

diabetes   leukemia   nephritis   multiple sclerosis

5. A vaccine can provide immunity against _____ .

tuberculosis   poliomyelitis   muscular dystrophy   cancer

6. One ailment that attacks the intestinal tract is _____ .

Parkinson's disease   mumps   angina   diarrhea

7. Which of the following is not transmitted through sexual contact?

AIDS   diabetes   gonorrhea   syphilis

8. A person who is sensitive to a certain substance is said to be allergic to it. Which of the following is not usually a sign of an allergy?

sneezing   a rash   difficult and/or noisy breathing   hiccups

9. Many varieties of _____ cause pain, swelling, and stiffness in the joints.

dysentery   dementia   rheumatism   diphtheria

10. Which one of the following is not an infectious condition?

tuberculosis   hay fever   polio   chickenpox

C. Write the medical meaning of each group of letters below.

PTA _____

PMS _____

AIDS _____

TB _____

D. Take a brief medical history of a friend or relative. Ask about past serious illnesses, accidents, and congenital defects. Ask about allergies, current medical problems, and medications taken regularly or occasionally. Take notes during the interview, and then write a paragraph about the state of the person's health.

E. Reread paragraph 5. What do these idioms mean?

cut down _____   cut out _____

V. CHECKING COMPREHENSION

Read each paragraph listed below. Then mark the following statements **T** (*true*) or **F** (*false*). Correct the false statements.

1. _____ [¶1] People don't contract infectious diseases very often anymore.

2. _____ [¶2] Life expectancy means how long the average person of a stated age is likely to live.

3. _____ [¶4] When part of the heart muscle dies, the patient dies, too.

4. _____ [¶6] Angina pectoris is a fatal condition.

5. _____ [¶11] Scientists know what causes all types of cancer.

6. _____ [¶14] Diabetes can be cured by taking insulin tablets.

7. _____ [¶19] Having a positive reaction to a TB test is good news for the patient.

CHAPTER 5

Physicians and Medical Specialties

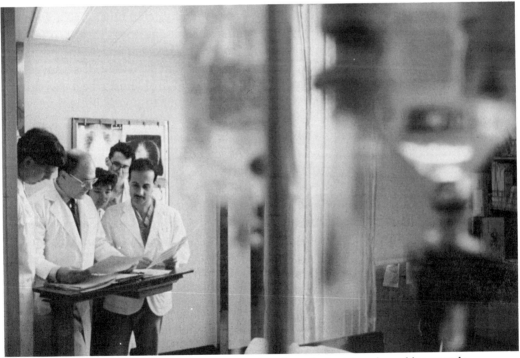

In a teaching hospital, interns often accompany experienced physicians in making rounds. (*Courtesy of Johns Hopkins Medical Institutions*)

1.   Modern medical care, especially in a hospital, is administered by a whole team of technically trained personnel. At the head of the team — supervising, making decisions, and writing the orders — is the physician.

2.   The professional life of a physician is not a dramatic tale of miraculous success and glory, as movies and TV often suggest. It is a rewarding and interesting life, but it is also physically and mentally exhausting, stressful, and full of great responsibility. In most countries, physicians enjoy at least a comfortable living as well as respect. However, they may also struggle through a 60- to 70-hour workweek and then be awakened at 4 A.M. to deal with a sudden emergency.

3.   In addition to medical knowledge and techniques, physicians need social skills in order to be successful with patients. Making an accurate diagnosis and determining appropriate treatment is only part of the job. After that, the physician must explain to the patient (in simple layman's terms) the nature of the condition. Next, the physician must give advice and sometimes offer alternatives. But what if the patient doesn't want to take the doctor's advice? The physician tries to persuade a self-indulgent patient to give up cigarettes or salt, convince a frightened patient that surgery is essential, or encourage a patient with emotional problems to seek psychiatric help. Sometimes it is necessary for the physician to give a patient very bad news, and this difficult task must be carried out with kindness and without destroying the patient's ability to face the future. In short, doctors who work directly with patients (and most do) need "people skills." The physician who can reassure and comfort a sick patient is said to have a good "bedside manner."

4.   In the United States, the training of a physician actually begins with what are called "pre-med" courses, the science and math classes required during undergraduate training for all who intend to apply to medical school. The curriculum includes biology and mathematics, biochemistry, organic and inorganic chemistry, and histology. Most students complete four years of undergraduate work before entering medical school, which takes another three or four years. After graduating from medical school, the student has earned the title *M.D.* (doctor of medicine). Those who graduate from a school of osteopathy receive a *D.O.* (doctor of osteopathy) and are also licensed to practice medicine after passing the state exam.

5.   An internship, or hands-on hospital training, is an essential part of a physician's training. In the past, a year of internship (rotating, supervised service in various hospital departments) followed medical school. Today, in many hospitals, a physician in training may serve as an **intern** during the final year of med school or the first year of a residency (specialty training). An internship in only one specialized service is called a "straight" internship.

6.   In order to practice medicine in a particular state, a physician must take that state's examination. Although there is reciprocity between most states, physicians who move to certain states may be required to pass the new state's medical examination in order to get a license to practice there.

7.   Most young physicians in the United States today choose to specialize. To become a **specialist,** a doctor must first receive training in an accredited program called a *residency*. This training takes from three to seven years, depending upon the field of specialization. Residency training takes place in a hospital or ambulatory care setting, where the specialist-in-training (called a **resident**) cares for patients under the supervision of experienced teacher-specialists. After completing the training, specialists may then take an examination given by the specialty board they are applying to. Those who pass are called *board-certified specialists.* In the United States, there are 24 specialties recognized by the American Board of Medical Specialties (ABMS) and the American Medical Association (AMA). Some specialty boards require physicians to practice in the specialty for a year or more before they may apply to become board certified.

8.   Some specialists later choose to subspecialize, which generally requires an additional two or more years of training. Two fields in which there are a number of **subspecialties** are internal medicine and pediatrics. General **internists** provide nonsurgical care for adolescents and adults. Internists may become subspecialists in thirteen different areas. Among these are cardiovascular medicine, gastroenterology, geriatric medicine (treatment of the elderly), hematology (diseases of the blood, spleen, and lymph glands), infectious diseases, nephrology (diseases of the kidney), pulmonary diseases, rheumatology (diseases of the joints, muscles, bones, and tendons), medical oncology (cancer), and allergy and immunology. **Pediatricians** (who treat children from birth to young adulthood) can subspecialize in seven different areas including cardiology, endocrinology, hematology-oncology, and neonatal-perinatal medicine.

9.   When choosing a specialty, physicians must consider many factors. One is, of course, which branch of medicine interests them most. Another practical consideration is need — which types of specialists are in short supply in the area where the physician plans to practice. But there are many other factors to consider. Physicians should choose fields that mesh best with their own abilities and talents. The first decision is whether one wants a surgical or a medical (nonsurgical) specialty. Internists and other medical specialists must be good diagnosticians, which requires the mental skills of a detective. Suppose a patient complains of frequent headaches. The cause might be anxiety or stress, sinus congestion, vision problems, a virus, a circulatory problem, a tumor, hypertension, or some other condition. The physician

treating this patient needs to know what questions to ask and what tests to order to find the cause.

10.   What characteristics must good surgeons have? Surgeons need good eye-hand coordination, manual dexterity, and (in some surgical specialties) the physical stamina to operate for several hours without rest. In addition to the specialty of **general surgery,** many other specialists do surgery on the part(s) of the body or type(s) of conditions they are trained to treat. Urologists, for instance, operate on the genitourinary system. Orthopedic surgeons (specialists in the skeletal-muscular system) operate on bones, muscles, and tendons. Thoracic surgeons operate on the chest. Included among their patients are people with coronary artery disease, **congenital anomalies,** or cancer of the lung or chest wall. Surgeons not only operate on their patients; they also provide perioperative care.

11.   Some physicians prefer to work in an operating room or a laboratory and interact more with medical personnel than with patients. Physicians who spend relatively little of their time talking and explaining to patients are **radiologists, anesthesiologists, pathologists,** and various types of researchers.

12.   A physician choosing a specialty must also consider this question: How willing am I to handle emergencies that interrupt my personal life? Some specialists, such as dermatologists (skin doctors) and **ophthalmologists** (eye doctors), have relatively few emergency calls. At the other end of the scale are allergists, obstetricians, pediatricians, and orthopedic surgeons, who must get used to middle-of-the-night phone calls due to asthma attacks, labor pains, high fevers, or broken bones. Many physicians will put up with the inconvenience of providing emergency care in order to work with basically healthy patients.

13.   Even in a medical specialty, the kinds of cases are often quite varied, involving both minor problems and major ones, both routine care and emergency treatment. Ophthalmologists, for example, may spend a lot of time in the office, seeing patients of all ages, doing routine vision and glaucoma tests. But they also deal with many older patients who have degenerative conditions and severe loss of vision. Ophthalmologists perform surgery for a wide variety of reasons, including "crossed" eyes, cataracts, detached retinas, and accidental injuries. An **otolaryngologist** (ear, nose, and throat specialist) might, in a single day, see patients with nasal polyps, sinusitis, hearing loss, and cancer of the larynx. On the other hand, some ENT specialists limit their practices and may do only rhinoplasties (plastic surgery on the nose) or stapedectomies (middle-ear surgery for hearing loss).

14.   There is some overlapping of care provided by the various specialties. A **rhinoplasty,** for example, might be done by an otolaryngologist or a plastic surgeon. A **hysterectomy** might be performed by a general surgeon

or by an **obstetrician-gynecologist.** Nasal allergies might be treated by an allergist or an otolaryngologist.

15. Medical specialization has helped to bring modern medical care to the high level that it is at today. In the world of contemporary medicine, where drugs and technology change rapidly, physicians who specialize bring much more experience and knowledge to the tasks of diagnosis and treatment. Medical research, too, has progressed with greater speed and success because of specialization.

16. But, for both physicians and patients, specialization has its disadvantages. Before specialization, the same doctor treated all the members of a family for all their problems. GPs (general practitioners) of the past knew their patients' medical histories and their family medical histories. Patients consulted one doctor who knew them well instead of a series of specialists who might not remember them from one visit to the next. Many physicians and patients feel that in this age of specialization, medical care is sometimes sadly impersonal.

17. For patients, another significant disadvantage of specialization is that a specialist providing medication for one condition might not monitor that drug's effect upon the patient in other ways, and adverse side effects may go unnoticed. For example, the ENT doctor who prescribes decongestants for sinus congestion may never notice that this medication has elevated the patient's blood pressure to abnormal limits. In addition, drugs prescribed by different specialists for the same person may turn out to be a poor combination.

18. Clearly, even in this age of specialization, patients need one physician following their general health and keeping track of all medical problems and medications being taken. When there is any question about the cause of a symptom, that primary physician is the one the patient should see first. (If Ellen Johnson wakes up with a pain in her side, she may not know whether the problem is in her muscles, kidneys, or lungs. She should consult her primary physician, who will refer her to a specialist, if necessary.) For children, the primary physician is often the pediatrician. For adults, it might be a **general practitioner** (GP), an internist, or a specialist in family practice.

19. Since contemporary medicine often offers more than one way to treat the same problem, it is quite common for patients to consult specialists for a second opinion. Sometimes the original physician suggests it, sometimes the patient wants it, and sometimes (especially when surgery is being considered) the patient's insurance company requires it before agreeing to pay for an expensive procedure.

20. Traditionally, American physicians have been self-employed solo practitioners. But today, many are salaried employees working for hospitals. Also, increasing numbers of doctors are associated with health maintenance

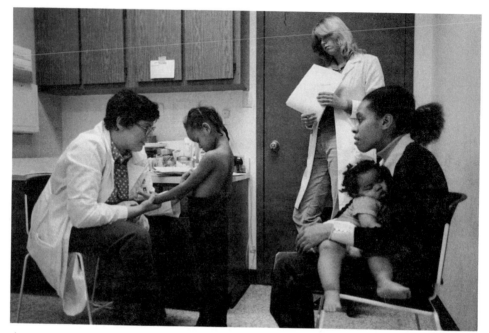

A general practitioner (GP), such as this physician in a family health care center, is prepared to treat all nonsurgical medical problems. (*Ken Karp*)

organizations (HMOs), organizations which provide health insurance and comprehensive health care to members. Physicians who are employed by or affiliated with a large group have the advantage of working only when they are on duty; they are less likely to be interrupted during their off-duty hours than physicians working alone or in small groups.

21.   In contrast, the life of physicians in solo private practice can be very hectic. Generally, they must go to at least two different locations in the course of a day: to their office to see patients and to the hospital they are affiliated with to make **rounds,** checking on their hospitalized patients and writing orders for their nursing care. Physicians in partnership practice may take turns with their colleagues, alternating nights and weekends "on call." Being on call means being totally available, and accepting the possibility of being called away from home to provide emergency care. At the very least, having an evening at home interrupted several times by calls from patients and hospital staff members is not unusual.

22.   All physicians, specialists or not, find that there can be no end to their education. They must keep up with new developments by reading journals, attending meetings, and sometimes learning to perform new types of operations or diagnostic procedures. The life of a physician has many rewards, but it is not easy. Anyone who chooses to enter the profession

must be prepared to accept the drawbacks and hardships along with the benefits.

SPECIAL TERMS

Physicians by Level of Training

general practitioner—a physician who treats all medical problems rather than specializing. Today, many GPs have completed a residency in family practice.

intern—member of a hospital staff receiving training in the practice of medicine by assisting attending physicians and physician teachers on a hospital staff. An internship may be completed during the final year of medical school, after graduation from medical school, or in conjunction with the first year of specialty training.

resident—a physician who continues clinical training after an internship. This is usually done as a member of the house staff of a hospital for the purpose of receiving training in a medical specialty.

specialist—a physician who, after receiving the M.D. degree, has completed the prescribed number of years of specialty training in an accredited residency program. A specialist who later passes an examination given by this specialty's board becomes a *board-certified specialist.*

subspecialist—a medical specialist who takes additional training in a branch of his specialty. For example, pediatric surgery is a subspecialty of general surgery; child psychiatry is a subspecialty of psychiatry; forensic (legal) pathology is a subspecialty of pathology; gynecologic oncology is a subspecialty of obstetrics-gynecology; geriatric medicine (treatment of the elderly) is one of several subspecialties of internal medicine. Subspecializing requires a year or more of additional full-time education in a program called a *fellowship.*

Some Medical Specialists

anesthesiologist—a specialist who provides pain relief and maintenance of a stable condition during a surgical, obstetric, or diagnostic procedure.

general surgeon—a specialist trained to perform a wide range of surgical procedures affecting most parts of the body. Some common procedures performed by a general surgeon are gall bladder removal (cholecystectomy), appendectomy, hernia repairs (herniorrhapy), and mastectomy.

internist—a specialist in internal medicine, trained to provide comprehensive nonsurgical care for adolescents and adults. Subspecialties in the field include geriatric medicine, infectious diseases, allergy, and oncology.

obstetrician-gynecologist—a specialist trained in the medical and surgical care of the female reproductive system. Subspecialties include maternal-fetal medicine and reproductive endocrinology (which deals with infertility problems).

ophthalmologist—a specialist who provides comprehensive eye and vision care, both medical and surgical.

otolaryngologist—a specialist trained to treat the ears, respiratory system, upper alimentary system, and head and neck in general. Commonly called an ear, nose, and throat (ENT) specialist.

pathologist—a specialist in the causes and nature of disease. Pathologists diagnose and monitor disease by microscopic examination of tissue specimens, cells, and body fluids and by performing laboratory tests on body fluids and secretions.

pediatrician—a medical specialist who treats children from birth to young adulthood. Subspecialties include pediatric oncology, allergy, endocrinology, nephrology, and cardiology.

radiologist—a medical specialist working in one of several branches of this field. Some of the branches are therapeutic radiology (also called radiation oncology, that is, the treatment of malignancies), diagnostic radiology, and nuclear radiology.

Surgical Procedures

hysterectomy—surgical removal of the uterus, often because of a benign or malignant tumor.

mastectomy—excision (surgical removal) of a breast.

rhinoplasty—plastic surgery of the nose.

Other Medical Vocabulary

anomaly — an organ or structure that is abnormal in its form, structure, or position.

congenital — present at birth.

rounds — doctors' visits to hospitalized patients. In teaching hospitals, attending physicians often make rounds accompanied by externs (medical students), interns, and residents.

VOCABULARY PRACTICE

1. What is the difference between a diagnostic radiologist and a therapeutic radiologist?

2. At what stage of a person's life is a congenital anomaly likely to be discovered?

3. What do the initials *GP* stand for?

4. Name four specialists who do not do surgery.

5. Which specialists in the vocabulary list commonly work in an operating room?

6. Which subspecialty deals with the treatment of elderly patients?

7. Can an internist subspecialize in a surgical specialty?

8. Do general practitioners ever complete residencies?

9. What is the difference between obstetrics and gynecology?

10. Which two specialists may subspecialize in allergies?

11. Which specialist, working in a laboratory, determines if a tumor is benign or malignant?

12. What is the difference between a *resident* and a *fellow*?

13. Who makes rounds in a hospital and why?

14. Which operation could be performed on a man: a hysterectomy or a rhinoplasty?

15. Is pediatric surgery a subspecialty of pediatrics or of general surgery?

EXERCISES

I. DISCUSSING MEDICAL MATTERS

1. What kinds of medical advice do patients often ignore? How can a physician encourage greater cooperation? Is this part of the physician's responsibility?

2. Should a physician be deeply concerned about what happens to patients? Is it possible to care too much?

3. Discuss the pros and cons of medical specialization.

4. If you were choosing a medical specialty, which one would you choose? Tell why that field appeals to you.

5. Which medical specialty would you be least likely to go into? Why?

II. ANALYZING WORDS AND WORD PARTS

A. Match each word part with its definition. Use a dictionary for help.

1. gastro-   _____ stomach

2. neo-   _____ child; foot

3. onco-   _____ mind

4. ophthalmo-   _____ new

5. ortho-   _____ tumor

6. oto-   _____ ear

7. ped-   _____ nose

8. psycho-   _____ straight

9. rhino-   _____ eye

10. thorac-   _____ chest

B. The word part *-plasty* means *repair*. What is the surgical procedure called a *rhinoplasty?* _____

What does a plastic surgeon do? _____

C. Use your knowledge of word parts to determine what kind of patients a *pediatric hematologist-oncologist* treats.

_____

D. What is the difference between:

1. *perinatal* and *prenatal* care? _____

_____

2. *preoperative, postoperative,* and *perioperative* care? _____

_____

3. an *incision* and an *excision*? _____

_____

III. PRONOUNCING MEDICAL AND GENERAL WORDS

A. **Practicing stress.** If a word ends in *-ology* or *-ologist,* when you say the word aloud, stress *-ol.* Say these words aloud:

cardiol′ogist   neurol′ogist   ophthalmol′ogist

otolaryngol′ogy   pathol′ogy   hematol′ogy

If a word ends with *-tric* or *-trics,* stress the preceding syllable. Say these words aloud:

pedia′trics   geria′trics   psychia′tric

B. **Hard *g* and soft *g*.** Pronounce the underlined letters as hard *g* [g]:

gynecology   gastroenterology

Pronounce the underlined letters as soft *g* [dʒ]:

geriatrics   gerontology

C. Say these words with *ph* pronounced [f]:

ophthalmologist   physical medicine   nephrologist

D.   The ending -*cian*.   Note that this ending is pronounced [ʃən], just as the letters *tion* are. Words that end with *-cian* are stressed on the preceding syllable. Say these words aloud:

physi′cian   diagnosti′cian   pediatri′cian   obstetri′cian

E.   Words that begin with *ps-* or *pn-*.   The *p* is always silent in these words. Say these words aloud:

psychiatrist   psychology   pneumonia   pneumatic

IV. USING NEW WORDS AND PHRASES

A.   What is the difference between an intern and an internist? _____

_____

B.   Why are physicians in training to become specialists called *residents?*

_____

_____

When you receive a piece of advertising in the mail addressed to "Resident," what does that mean? _____

_____

C.   Read the statements below. Then identify the physician's purpose in making each statement to a patient: to suggest, to explain, to advise, to warn, or to reassure.

  1. Drinking alcoholic beverages is likely to increase the frequency and severity of your dizzy spells. _____

  2. The bony growth in your middle ear is what's causing your hearing loss. _____

  3. This certainly looks and feels like a benign tumor. We'll do a biopsy on it just to be sure, but don't be alarmed about it.

_____

4. If you exercise more, your legs will get stronger, and you'll feel better. _____

5. Our nursing staff will be watching you closely, and I'll prescribe enough pain medication to give you substantial relief.

_____

D. Below is a list of the medical specialties. Choose from this list to identify the specialist(s) likely to handle each situation below.

allergist and immunologist

anesthesiologist

colon and rectal surgeon

dermatologist

emergen‸y physician

family practice physician

internist

neurological surgeon

neurologist

nuclear medicine specialist

obstetrician-gynecologist

ophthalmologist

orthopedic surgeon

otolaryngologist

pathologist

pediatrician

physiatrist

plastic surgeon

preventive medicine physician

psychiatrist

radiologist

general surgeon

thoracic surgeon

urologist

1. Juan Rodriguez fell out of a tree. Now his arm hurts. Which specialist can read the X-ray and determine if the arm is broken?

_____ If there is a fracture, which specialist should Juan see? _____

2. George Lewis flunked out of law school last week, and since then, he's been too depressed to get out of bed. Which specialist should his family consult? _____

3. Ilya Freyman's TV antenna punctured a hole in his eardrum, leaving him with a substantial hearing loss. Which specialist should he consult? _____

4. Mona Patel has a rash on her hands. It itches and stings. Which specialist can help? _____

5. During the late summer, Young Ran Kim sneezes about 200 times a day. Name two specialists who might treat her for this common problem. _____

_____

6. Sofia Miller felt a lump in her breast. Which doctors might she go to for an opinion about what to do next?

_____   _____

7. José Perez had an emergency appendectomy last week. Who probably operated on him? _____

8. George Jones was murdered last week. The specialist performing the autopsy to determine the cause of death is a forensic

_____.

9. Boris Rothman went to a health fair and had his blood pressure taken. He was told that it was elevated and that he should see a doctor. Which specialist did he probably consult?

_____

After each of the 24 specialists listed above, mark an *S* if this specialist does surgery or an *M* if this specialist is a medical specialist.

E.   Complete each sentence below with one of the expressions listed.

give up	second opinion	on duty	on call
keep up	side effect	off duty	make rounds

1. Dr. Anh Vo can't go away from home tonight unless he takes his pager with him because he's _____ tonight.

2. Whenever Tatyana Treyger takes antibiotics, she gets severe stomach cramps. That's an adverse _____.

3. The residents in that hospital work very hard. Every other night, they are _____ and must sleep at the hospital.

4. Dr. Shotz is a busy surgeon and has several hospitalized patients all the time. Every day, he goes to the hospital in the late afternoon to _____ and write orders regarding the postoperative care of his patients.

5. When patients are obese, doctors ask them to _____ eating foods that are very fattening.

V. CHECKING COMPREHENSION

A. Mark each statement below **T** (*true*) or **F** (*false*). Correct the statements that are false.

_____ **1.** Physicians cannot practice as specialists until they become board certified.

_____ **2.** Physicians become specialists by completing accredited residency programs.

_____ **3.** Physicians must become specialists before they can begin training in a subspecialty.

_____ **4.** Internists perform surgery on the internal organs.

_____ **5.** Specialists in geriatrics deliver babies.

_____ **6.** The phrase *practicing medicine* means learning how to be a physician.

_____ **7.** According to ¶9 and ¶10, it's more difficult to be a surgeon than a medical specialist.

B. According to this chapter, what are some of the disadvantages of being a physician? Can you think of any other disadvantages in addition to the ones mentioned here? What are some advantages?

Review Exercises (Chapters 1-5)

I.   Complete the sentences below with words from the following list.

acute	chronic	infarction
atrophy	cure	prognosis
cadaver	hemorrhaging	syndrome

1. What's the _____, doctor? Can you

    _____ this patient, or is she terminally ill?

2. An appendicitis attack is an _____ medical problem. Nasal allergies, on the other hand, are usually a

    _____ problem.

3. A _____ is a group of symptoms that occur together.

4. Muscles _____ if they are not used.

5. If we can't stop this patient's excessive bleeding

    (_____), he'll soon be a _____
    (corpse) instead of a patient.

II.   Do the following words refer to something found inside the body? Mark each word **Y** (*yes*) or **N** (*no*).

_____ atria	_____ gland	_____ pathogen
_____ cough	_____ nausea	_____ stroke
_____ epidermis	_____ paralysis	_____ uterus

III. Match each word part with its definition. Use a dictionary for help.

1. ab-   _____ across; between; through

2. di-   _____ difficult; bad

3. dia-   _____ fungus

4. dys-   _____ hard

5. hist-   _____ near or beside; abnormal

6. hypo-   _____ abnormal or diseased condition

7. mal-   _____ under; below normal

8. myc-   _____ double; twice; two

9. -osis   _____ away; from

10. para-   _____ tissue

11. peri-   _____ bad; ill

12. scler-   _____ around

IV. Next to the common name, write the formal name for each medical specialist or subspecialist described below.

1. cancer specialist _____

2. children's doctor _____

3. ear, nose, and throat doctor _____

4. eye doctor _____

5. heart specialist _____

6. skin doctor _____

V. Write the meanings of the following abbreviations:

EEG _____

ENT _____

GP _____

HIV _____

IV _____

OB _____

PMS _____

STD _____

TB _____

VI. Discuss the meanings of the following phrases:

1. booster shot

2. case history

3. gross anatomy

4. life expectancy

5. make rounds

6. over the counter

7. tentative diagnosis

8. treatment of choice

9. trial and error

VII. As a group, take the medical history of a volunteer classmate, a visitor, or your teacher. Take turns asking the "patient" about:

1. age

2. marital status and number of children

3. past illnesses

4. past accidents

5. recent hospitalizations

6. present medical problems

7. medications taken regularly

8. parents' health

9. health of other family members

10. amount of exercise

11. level of stress

12. smoking habits

13. alcoholic consumption

Some of your questions should begin with *Do you . . . ? Have you ever . . . ? How often do you . . . ? What medications (diseases, etc.) . . . ?*

VIII. Underline the correct answer to complete each statement.

1. About which medical specialist do you think people jokingly say, "He never kills his patients, and he never cures them"? **(a)** cardiologist; **(b)** dermatologist; **(c)** general surgeon; **(d)** pediatrician.

2. Which specialist jokingly warns his patients, "Never put anything smaller than your elbow into your ear"? **(a)** ophthalmologist; **(b)** obstetrician; **(c)** otolaryngologist; **(d)** oncologist.

CHAPTER 6

Surgery

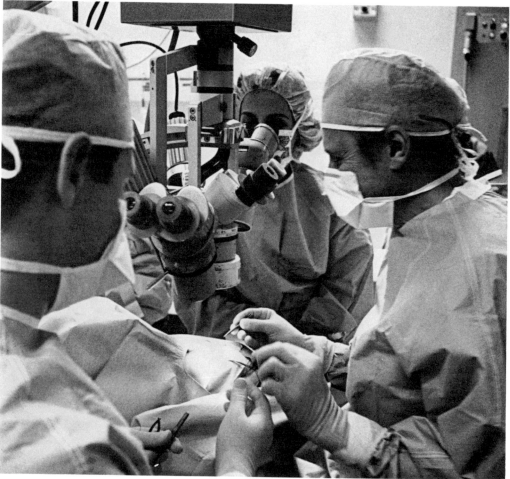

Eye surgery with the help of microscopes is one example of the sophisticated surgical techniques now in use. (*Laima E. Druskis*)

1.   One of the most dramatic medical procedures is surgery. Ever since ancient times, people have tried to cure medical problems by cutting into the body. Surgical operations are depicted on the tombs of the Egyptian Pharaohs, dating from 3000 B.C. These early operations were painful and hazardous. If an **amputation** was necessary, for example, alcohol was often used to dull the pain somewhat, but the patient did not have the benefit of an effective anesthetic drug. And after the surgery was performed, there was great risk of infection because the use of antiseptics was unknown.

2.   Today, operations are performed under **sterile** conditions, and great care is taken during and after each **operation** to avoid infection. A variety of anesthetic drugs are available to make the patient pain-free during the operation, and highly trained medical specialists (anesthesiologists) can determine the proper drug and dosage to use. Many operations which used to require lengthy hospital stays are now performed under local anesthetic, often on an **outpatient** basis. Hernia repair (herniorrhaphy), hemorrhoidectomy, and cataract removal are some of the operations that have been dramatically improved in recent years. Greater precision and smaller incisions greatly decrease the risk and pain of surgery as well as the recuperation period and cost.

3.   In recent years, major advances have been made. Operations are now performed that were not even imagined 30 years ago. Clogged blood vessels can be cleaned out or replaced. Kidneys, livers, and even hearts and lungs can be transplanted from one person to another. Heart valves are routinely replaced, and severed limbs sewn back onto the body.

4.   These sophisticated operations require extremely skilled and experienced physicians. Most surgeons concentrate on learning and practicing in one area of surgery. An orthopedic surgeon, for example, repairs or replaces broken or damaged bones, while a neurosurgeon handles surgery involving the nervous system. A plastic surgeon repairs or replaces defects of form and function, most commonly on the skin, head, limbs, breasts, and external genitalia. A thoracic surgeon operates on patients with chest and respiratory ailments. General surgeons operate mostly on the abdominal organs, breasts, and endocrine glands.

5.   Most patients are referred to a surgeon by their regular internist or family physician, who has recognized the possible need for surgical involvement. After examining the patient and the medical records from the patient's physician, the surgeon must determine whether surgery is needed and can improve the patient's condition without undue risk. Sometimes, **exploratory surgery** must be done to determine whether **corrective surgery** should be undertaken.

6.   Surgery may be classified as emergency, urgent, required, elective, or optional. Emergency surgery is done when there is a life-threatening crisis

which demands immediate action (for example, a tracheotomy, which is done to enable a patient to breathe). Urgent surgery requires prompt but not immediate action. Required surgery is that which the patient needs to cure a particular health problem but which can be postponed for weeks or months. **Elective surgery** can correct a condition but is not necessary to the health of the patient (for example, middle-ear surgery to correct a hearing loss). Optional surgery is done primarily for cosmetic rather than health reasons. Exploratory surgery is performed for diagnostic purposes.

7. A patient about to undergo surgery is instructed not to eat or drink anything for several hours prior to the operation in order to make it easier for the surgeon to operate and to avoid complications from the anesthetic. A patient is often given an enema just before the operation to void the colon of waste material. Sometimes, a urinary **catheter** is used to drain the bladder. The area to be operated on is shaved and scrubbed with soap, and an antiseptic is applied to avoid infection.

8. The patient is then wheeled into the operating room and placed on the operating table. A blood pressure cuff is attached to one arm just above the elbow to measure the blood pressure at regular intervals, and an **intravenous (IV) line** attached to a catheter is inserted into the other arm. This allows intravenous solution to be given to help maintain the body fluids and also to provide a way to administer essential drugs during the operation. The site of the operation is *draped* (sterile sheets placed around the operation site), leaving an opening at the incision area. A mask may be placed over the patient's mouth and nose, or a tube may be placed in the **trachea** through which a general anesthetic and oxygen are given. Some types of anesthetic drugs are administered directly with a hypodermic needle. Donated blood of the same type as the patient's may be on hand in case a transfusion becomes necessary.

9. The surgeon is assisted by a large staff. There is usually an assistant surgeon or two, who are probably interns or residents. The patient's physician may also be present. The chief operating-room nurse supervises the operating-room nursing staff, which includes a scrub nurse in charge of surgical supplies and equipment; a circulating nurse, not dressed in a sterile gown, who is in charge of activities outside the sterile theater; and an orderly to help move the patient.

10. An important member of the surgical team is the anesthesiologist. This specialist is responsible for administering the anesthetic that renders the patient insensible of pain during the operation. Great care must be taken to provide enough anesthetic to keep the patient unconscious, yet not so much that it will dangerously lower the patient's respiration, pulse, or blood pressure. The patient's history of allergies must also be considered in determining the type of anesthetic that is to be used. Anesthetics probably present the greatest risk to the patient during an operation. Improper use could

cause severe allergic reaction resulting in **shock** or cardiac or respiratory arrest.

11.   Surgery requires a large variety of specialized equipment. In addition to the special operating table, there are high-intensity lights and the anesthesia machine. A main instrument table is covered with a large collection of **scalpels, forceps, suture** needles, **retractors,** and other instruments. There are vacuum machines to suck out excess blood and other fluids from the part of the body being operated upon. Containers of blood and dextrose are on hand. There are wash basins and refuse bins. A special **sponge** stand holds the used sponges (cotton pads used for mopping blood).

12.   An operation may be completed in less than an hour, or it may last for several hours. Before the patient is sewn up, the used sponges and the instruments are always counted by the circulating nurse and one other person to ensure that none have been left inside the patient's body. Once surgery is completed, careful postoperative care is begun. The wound is carefully bandaged, and the **dressings** are changed frequently. The patient is wheeled into a recovery room and kept there until awakening from the

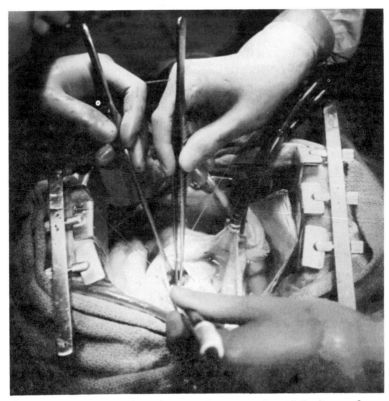

Forceps, retractors, and suction machines are a few of the items of specialized equipment used in surgery. (*Mark Mellett*)

anesthetic. Often, the patient is then taken to an intensive care unit, where the **vital signs** are carefully monitored. Once out of danger, the patient is taken to a hospital room or ward. Early **ambulation** is prescribed to prevent blood clots and bed sores. When the services of the hospital staff and equipment are no longer needed, the patient is returned home or to an intermediate-care facility, where recuperation is completed.

13.   During the first few days after surgery, a routine is followed which helps to prevent many of the problems that have killed surgical patients in the past. The hospital room is kept as sterile as possible through the use of antiseptics. Pneumonia is prevented by antibiotics and respiratory therapy. The development of embolisms (clots which form in a blood vessel and travel to other, critical sites) is reduced by early postoperative ambulation. And shock, which used to be the most common cause of postoperative death, is held to a minimum by the use of blood and plasma transfusion.

14.   Another risk associated with surgery is human error. A patient trusts the surgeon to be competent and conscientious and presumes that everything possible will be done to make the operation a success. But mistakes may happen which result in serious injury to the patient. Hospitals and most medical professionals carry **medical malpractice** (professional liability) insurance to compensate the patient for any injury resulting from negligence.

15.   Although modern surgery can produce amazing results with minimal risk, the benefits are likely to carry a huge price tag. Despite a substantial reduction in the number of days one spends in a hospital for an operation, even the simplest surgery is likely to cost many thousands of dollars when taking into account the cost of the hospital room, the operating room, the anesthesiologist's charge, and the surgeon's fee, along with the expenses for drugs and equipment. People not covered by medical insurance can have their savings wiped out by the costs of surgery and related medical care.

SPECIAL TERMS

Some Reasons for Surgery

corrective surgery — surgery in which the aim is to treat the problem.

elective surgery — a surgical procedure that need not be performed immediately and can therefore be planned at the patient's convenience; an operation that is not essential for the patient's survival.

exploratory surgery—surgery performed for diagnostic purposes, to discover the nature or extent of the problem.

Operating Room Equipment and Instruments

catheter—a tube for evacuating or injecting fluids, often used to give patients water, blood, or medication during surgery; also used to remove urine.

dressing—a protective or supportive covering for a wound.

forceps—an instrument for holding, grabbing, or extracting. (There are many different types for different surgical procedures.)

intravenous line—a method of getting life-saving fluids and/or medication directly into the patient's vein. (Often, a catheter is used to create this line.)

retractors—instruments for holding back the margins of a wound; used to hold the surgical site open during an operation.

scalpel—a small, straight surgical knife with a convex edge on its thin, very sharp blade.

sponge—an absorbent pad made of gauze and cotton, commonly used in surgery to absorb blood.

sutures—another name for the stitches used in sewing up the opening (incision) after an operation.

Other Medical Vocabulary

ambulation—walking about; moving of one's own volition. Early ambulation is encouraged after surgery to prevent complications such as a blood clot.

amputation—the cutting off of part of the body; a surgical procedure that may be necessary due to disease or infection.

medical malpractice—improper or negligent treatment of a patient. Patients sometimes sue physicians, claiming malpractice, so most physicians have malpractice insurance.

operation—a surgical procedure; cutting into the body for medical reasons.

outpatient — a patient who receives treatment at a hospital but is not hospitalized overnight.

shock — a clinical syndrome involving a disturbance of the oxygen supply to tissues and the return of blood to the heart. During surgery, shock may be caused by hemorrhage, hypotension (low blood pressure), respiratory failure, cardiac irregularity, or stroke.

sterile — perfectly clean; germ-free. All surgical instruments must be sterilized to avoid infection.

trachea — a tube going from the larynx (voice box) to the bronchial tubes; commonly called the windpipe. During surgery, a tube may be placed in the trachea to administer anesthetic or oxygen.

vital signs — indications of functions essential to life. Blood pressure, pulse, rate of respiration, and temperature are the major vital signs.

VOCABULARY PRACTICE

1. What do surgeons call an operation that is performed in order to determine the cause of a patient's symptoms?

2. What is an *outpatient?*

3. What things in an operating room must be sterile?

4. During surgery, what is a sponge used for?

5. What instrument is used to make an incision at the beginning of an operation?

6. What instrument would a surgeon be likely to use to remove a sponge from the surgical site?

7. During surgery, what are retractors used for?

8. What are the major vital signs essential to human life that must be monitored during surgery?

9. Why might a patient go into shock during surgery?

10. What are some uses of catheters during operations?

11. Which one is a surgical procedure: ambulation or amputation?

12. What do surgeons use to sew up the patient's incision after surgery?

13. After the surgical incision has been closed, what is often put over it?

14. Whom does malpractice insurance protect?

15. If a patient has a hearing loss and the physician says that surgery might improve the patient's hearing, would the operation be considered corrective or elective or both?

EXERCISES

I. DISCUSSING MEDICAL MATTERS

1. What are some general reasons why physicians recommend surgery to patients?

2. How is a patient prepared for major surgery? Discuss what happens from the time of hospital admission to the time that the patient is wheeled into the operating room.

3. Once the patient is in the operating room, what happens immediately prior to surgery? Discuss preparations for anesthesia, monitoring vital signs, and creating a germ-free environment.

4. What kinds of things can happen during surgery that might leave the medical personnel or the hospital vulnerable to a malpractice suit?

5. Discuss a surgical procedure that you have had or are familiar with. Was it major or minor surgery? Was it done as an outpatient or inpatient? Tell what type of physician performed the surgery, the length of the operation, the type of anesthetic used, the length and type of postoperative care needed, and the length of recuperation.

II. ANALYZING WORDS AND WORD PARTS

A. The suffixes at the top of page 80 indicate types of surgical procedures. On the line next to each word part, write its meaning. On the next line, write a surgical procedure ending with that suffix.

	Meaning	Surgical Procedure
1. -ectomy	_____	_____
2. -rrhaphy	_____	_____
3. -stomy	_____	_____
4. -tomy	_____	_____

B.   Write a definition for each pair of word parts below.

1. intra- _____   inter- _____

2. pre- _____   post- _____

C.   Negative prefixes are word parts that are used at the beginning of a word and add the meaning *not*. Some negative prefixes are *a-, ab-, an-, ir-, il-, in-, im-, non-,* and *un-*. Add the correct negative prefix to each word or word part below.

1. _____ esthesia   **5.** _____ normal

2. _____ septic   **6.** _____ sensible

3. _____ proper   **7.** _____ conscious

4. _____ regular   **8.** _____ oxia

III. PRONOUNCING MEDICAL AND GENERAL WORDS

A.   The letter *c* is usually pronounced [s] when it comes before the letters *e, i,* or *y*. It is pronounced [k] most other times. *Ch* is also sometimes pronounced [k]. Say the following words aloud.

[s]	[k]	
forceps	catheter	trachea
thoracic	scalpel	cure
certified	cataract	scrub

B.   The letter *x* is sometimes pronounced [ks] and sometimes [gz]. Say the following words aloud with the help of the pronunciation symbols following each.

examine [gz]   extra [ks]

exit [gz]   oxygen [ks]

Say the following pair of words aloud: sick/six

C. It is important to make a distinction between the sounds [s] and [ʃ]. Say these pairs of words aloud. (The underlined letters are pronounced [ʃ].)

science/conscientious   save/shave   sock/shock

surgeon/ensure   suture/shoe   space/specialist

D. Read the following sentences aloud. Pay attention to the stress marks.

1. He had a severe' illness.

2. The surgeon accidentally sev'ered an artery.

3. The patient refused' to sign the papers giving the surgeon permission to operate.

4. They threw the ref'use into the ref'use bin.

IV. USING NEW WORDS AND PHRASES

A. What is each of the items below used for during surgery? Write the answers.

1. catheter _____

2. drape _____

3. dressing _____

4. forceps _____

5. retractor _____

6. scalpel _____

7. sponge _____

8. suture _____

B.   Discuss the answers to the following questions in class.

1. What parts of the body are sometimes amputated because of severe, uncontrollable infection?

2. What categories of surgery can be postponed? What categories of surgery must be performed immediately or within a few days or weeks?

3. What is *cosmetic surgery?*

4. What do health-care workers mean when they talk about *complications* that a patient has developed?

5. What is the difference between the administration of a hospital and the administration of a drug?

6. What is the difference between plastic tubing and plastic surgery?

V. CHECKING COMPREHENSION

Reread each paragraph cited to find the context of each italicized word or phrase. Then underline the correct completion to each sentence below.

1. In ¶6, the word *enable* means **(a)** make it possible, allow; **(b)** encourage; **(c)** make it impossible.

2. In ¶7, the word *avoid* means **(a)** prevent; **(b)** encourage; **(c)** undergo.

3. In ¶7, the word *void* means **(a)** fill; **(b)** contain; **(c)** empty.

4. In ¶9, the phrase *circulating nurse* means **(a)** an orderly; **(b)** an aseptic nurse; **(c)** a nurse who is not directly involved in the surgical procedure.

5. In ¶9, the word *theater* means **(a)** a place where a play is performed; **(b)** the operating room, which may also have seating for observers; **(c)** an area for outpatient surgery.

6. In ¶9, the word *orderly* means **(a)** neat and in the proper place; **(b)** an assistant in the operating room; **(c)** a person who orders others around.

7. In ¶10, the word *insensible* means **(a)** lacking in good judgment or common sense; **(b)** stupid; **(c)** unable to feel.

8. In the first sentence of ¶12, the word *last* means **(a)** continue; **(b)** finish; **(c)** occur after all other activities.

9. In ¶12, sentence 2, the word *ensure* means **(a)** to be certain; **(b)** find out if; **(c)** to provide.

10. In the last sentence of ¶13, the phrase *used to* means **(a)** it was common; **(b)** true in the past but not now; **(c)** true in the past and still true.

11. In the last sentence of ¶15, the idiom *wiped out* means **(a)** cleaned carefully with a cloth; **(b)** invested; **(c)** lost, taken from them.

CHAPTER 7

Careers in Health Care

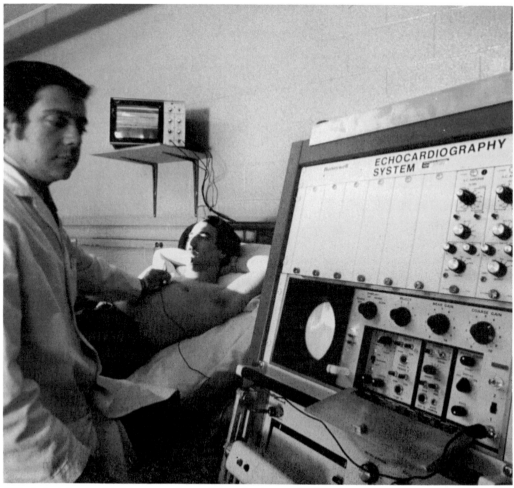

This technician is obtaining an *echocardiograph*, the result of a procedure that uses sound waves to form a picture of the internal structures of the heart.

fisichian

1. The medical profession has progressed considerably since the days when barbers performed surgery. Physicians are highly trained and educated, and they rely upon many other medical professionals to do tasks that don't require the skill of a medical doctor. **Technological** advances have greatly increased the need for persons trained in a wide variety of health-related occupations. These **paramedical** (or allied health) personnel are well trained to do their jobs. Depending upon the function, that training can be received on the job, or it may require as much as two years of training beyond a bachelor's degree.

2. The most familiar paramedical personnel are nurses, who perform both in and out of the hospital. Being a nurse does not require as many years of study as a doctor, but one must be equally dedicated. Caring for sick people demands great patience and a lot of work.

3. Nurses assist in the operating room and attend to the medical needs of hospitalized patients in accordance with doctors' orders. Some nurses are employed in physicians' offices to do preliminary examinations of patients and other duties that do not require the physicians' personal attention. There are two types of nurses — registered nurses (RNs) and licensed practical nurses (LPNs). To become a registered nurse usually requires at least a high school diploma plus two years of college or **vocational** school nursing courses. There are also college programs in nursing (leading to a bachelor's degree) which take four to five years to complete. Registered nurses have the major responsibility for patient care, acting upon the written direction of the physician. Practical nurses can be certified after one year of post-high-school study, but they earn less money and are given fewer technical responsibilities than registered nurses. Nurses work in all medical settings — hospitals, nursing homes, extended care facilities, outpatient clinics, physicians' offices, and private homes.

4. **Electrocardiograph** and **electroencephalograph technicians** operate diagnostic machines. The electrocardiograph (EKG) machine measures the electrical impulses that occur when the heart beats. The operator attaches **electrodes** to the chest, arms, and legs of the patient, and the machine makes a paper record (electrocardiogram) of the various responses, which are later read and **interpreted** by a physician. The electroencephalograph (EEG) records brain waves in a manner similar to the electrocardiograph. The electrodes are placed on the patient's head, and the recording is made while the patient is at rest. Many EKG technicians are trained on the job, while EEG technicians require one or two years of training in a hospital program, vocational school, or college.

5. Dialysis technicians operate hemodialysis machines, which take the place of a patient's damaged kidneys. Patients requiring dialysis receive treatments three times a week to relieve their blood of the waste products

that have collected. Dialysis technicians are normally trained on the job. They may work in a hospital, physician's office, or dialysis center.

6.   There are three types of radiologic technicians. Diagnostic technicians take and develop X-rays. They must also be able to read the X-rays to the extent of knowing whether or not the X-ray clearly shows the areas ordered by the physician. Radiation therapy technicians provide radiation to patients in order to destroy tumors or other foreign tissue. **Nuclear** medicine technicians introduce **radioactive** materials into the patient's bloodstream for diagnosis or treatment of disease or injury. The radioactive substance permits sophisticated X-ray machines to make photographic images of organs that would not be visible using ordinary X-ray techniques. X-ray technicians require a two- to four-year course in radiography after graduation from high school. Most radiation technicians work in hospitals, although some diagnostic technicians may be employed by physicians or **chiropractor**s.

7.   Occupational therapists use patient activity in order to help patients recover from physical, mental, or emotional **disability.** For instance, sewing may be prescribed to help develop fine motor functions that may have been lost because of stroke or **trauma.** Exercises to develop atrophied or injured muscles are also employed. Occupational therapy requires a high school diploma, two years of college, plus an additional two-year training program. Some colleges offer four-year programs in occupational therapy.

8.   Like occupational therapists, physical therapists work directly with patients, using exercise, heat, massage, and other physical means to **alleviate** pain and/or overcome disabilities. A four-year college degree in physical therapy qualifies one for this career.

9.   Both physical and occupational therapists act under the general direction of a physician but prescribe the specific courses of treatment themselves. There are also occupational and physical therapists' aides who can work with patients to help them perform the activities prescribed by the therapist.

10.   **Inhalation** therapists help people with respiratory ailments (such as asthma, bronchitis, and emphysema) to breathe. They operate various kinds of respirators and oxygen tents and administer the medication prescribed by the physician.

11.   One of the newest of medical careers is that of the physician assistant. Physician assistants (commonly called PAs) work under the supervision of a physician and can perform many of the functions of a physician, including certain types of minor surgery. They are licensed and regulated by the various states, and their duties and responsibilities are determined by state laws. Of course, these are jobs which demand substantial training. At

least two years of college plus two years of vocational training are usually required.

12.   Emergency medical technicians, sometimes called *paramedics,* operate mobile medical facilities, which are equipped to provide emergency medical care to patients away from a hospital and to transport them to a medical facility. Paramedics are trained to deliver cardiopulmonary **resuscitation** (CPR) to a patient who is not breathing or whose heart has stopped. They also provide intravenous injections and blood transfusions when necessary. Many emergency vehicles are equipped with a telephone line to the emergency room of a hospital so that paramedics can get instructions from a physician as to the treatment to be provided. These telephone lines can also be used to transmit electrocardiograms from the remote scene where the patient is located to the emergency room physician so that a proper diagnosis can be made and a course of emergency treatment provided. Once the patient is sufficiently **stabilized,** the paramedics transport the patient to the emergency room to be examined and treated by a physician.

13.   There are many careers that do not require as much education or training as the primary paramedical assistants (such as technicians or therapists). Nurses' aides assist nurses by performing routine chores. Hospital orderlies clean, dress, and move patients who are not ambulatory. And there are EKG and EEG aides who assist the technicians by preparing patients for administration of the tests. These positions require no more than on-the-job training.

14.   There are also many highly skilled medical personnel who are not primarily employed by hospitals. Pharmacists dispense drugs upon the orders (prescriptions) of physicians. They also advise customers about nonprescription drugs and possible side effects or adverse reactions to drugs. Many pharmacists keep a record of all medications being taken by a customer so that they can alert the customer if the combination of drugs being taken could produce an adverse reaction. Laboratory technicians work with microscopes, **centrifuges,** and other laboratory instruments, examining and analyzing samples of tissue, blood, urine, or other body fluids sent by physicians for diagnostic purposes.

15.   Other types of medical professionals who are not M.D.'s are trained in a particular area of medicine. **Podiatrists** treat people with foot problems and can perform minor surgery within their area of specialization. **Optometrists** examine eyes and prescribe corrective lenses, when necessary. Chiropractors and naprapaths treat the skeletal-muscular system by adjusting bones or joints and using heat and massage to relax tightened muscles.

16.   There are literally hundreds of careers in medicine. Some involve direct contact with sick or injured patients. Others involve working in a

Doing blood tests and writing up the reports are some of the tasks handled by lab technicians. (*Laima E. Druskis*)

laboratory doing research or analyzing tissue. One can find a medical career at almost any level of education and training.

SPECIAL TERMS

Vocabulary Relating to Allied Health Occupations

chiropractor — a practitioner who treats patients by manipulation of the vertebrae of the spinal column. (The word *chiropractic* comes from the Greek and means *effective hand*.) Chiropractors are not M.D.'s but have a D.C. (doctor of chiropractic) degree.

optometrist — a specialist who diagnoses problems relating to vision and prescribes corrective lenses to improve vision. The optometrist is not an M.D.

paramedical — relating to the treatment of medical problems by trained personnel assisting or acting upon the direction of a physician.

podiatrist — a practitioner whose training and treatment is limited to minor problems of the foot. (The podiatrist is not an M.D.)

technician — a person trained to operate machinery in a laboratory or to work with patients needing laboratory tests or other diagnostic procedures.

vocational — pertaining to a job, career, or profession.

Vocabulary Relating to Equipment Used for Treatment or Diagnosis

centrifuge — a machine that separates the different components of a liquid by the use of centrifugal force (material spinning at high speed). It is used for various lab tests.

electrocardiograph — a machine that measures electrical impulses caused by the beating of the heart. The information is then shown on a line graph (commonly called an EKG), which is produced as the heart beats.

electrode — a device (attached to an electrical wire) that can detect electrical impulses and transmit the information to a machine which graphically displays the information for analysis.

electroencephalograph — a machine similar to the electrocardiograph except that the information comes from the brain. (The resulting line graph is called an EEG.)

nuclear — pertaining to the energy produced by the nucleus of an atom. In medicine, the term relates to the use of radioactive isotopes for diagnosis or treatment of disease.

radioactive — emitting radiant energy from certain elements such as radium, plutonium, uranium, etc. Radioactive materials are used in X-ray and nuclear medicine technology.

technological — pertaining to the use of scientific knowledge. (See Chapter 9 relating to medical technology.)

Vocabulary Relating to Medical Problems

disability – a difficulty or inability of a bodily function to perform properly. Blindness, deafness, and paralysis are all examples of disabilities.

trauma – a physical or mental injury.

Vocabulary Relating to Diagnosis and Treatment

alleviate – lessen the pain or symptoms of an illness or injury.

inhalation – the act of drawing air into the lungs.

interpret – to explain data in practical terms. A physician interprets an electrocardiogram by reading the graph produced by the machine and translating the information, determining whether the graph shows pathology and, if so, what specific problem is indicated.

resuscitation – reviving a person's arrested (stopped) heartbeat or breathing.

stabilize – treating patients until they are out of immediate danger. Examples are obtaining normal vital signs and correcting bleeding or breathing difficulties.

VOCABULARY PRACTICE

1. What is the difference between the job of an optometrist and that of a podiatrist?

2. Compare and contrast the optometrist and the ophthalmologist. (See Chapter 5 to review information about the ophthalmologist.)

3. What is the difference between a paramedical career and a medical career?

4. Which part of the body is checked by an EEG and which by an EKG?

5. In what ways are these two diagnostic procedures similar?

6. What is the difference between an X-ray and an EEG?

7. Who interprets an EEG or an EKG – the patient, the X-ray technician, or a physician?

8. What does the term *nuclear medicine* mean?

9. If an elderly patient is very hard of hearing (almost deaf), you can call this problem a handicap or a _____.

10. What kinds of problems do physicians want to alleviate?

11. Give some examples of *trauma*.

12. What kinds of information must a physician interpret?

13. What is a common word that means *to inhale and exhale?*

14. Name some common physical disabilities.

15. Give some examples of ways in which modern technology assists physicians in the diagnosis and treatment of patients.

EXERCISES

I. DISCUSSING MEDICAL MATTERS

1. Name some allied health workers who perform important functions in a hospital.

2. Discuss the words *occupation, vocation, career,* and *profession.* Are any of them synonyms? How do they differ in meaning? Which one(s) do you think best describe the nurse, the pharmacist, the inhalation therapist, and the nurse's aide?

3. Name some allied health practitioners who work in an operating room. Tell what tasks each performs.

4. Which allied health workers deal mostly with emergencies? Discuss some emergency procedures that these allied health workers may perform on patients whose lives are in immediate danger.

II. ANALYZING WORDS AND WORD PARTS

Use a medical dictionary or a large general dictionary to help you answer the questions on pages 92 and 93.

A. vivi-

1. What does the word part *vivi-* mean? _____

2. In a medical setting, what does the word *revive* mean? _____

   _____

3. What is its more general meaning? _____

4. What does the word *vivacious* mean? _____

5. What is vivisection? _____

B. par- / para- / -para

1. What are the various meanings of these word parts?

   par- _____

   para- _____

   -para _____

2. What is a *paramedic?* _____

3. What are *paramedical careers?* _____

   _____

4. What is *paraplegia?* _____

5. What is *paranoia?* _____

C. dis-

1. What are the various meanings of the word part *dis-?* _____

   _____

2. What is the literal meaning of the word *disease?* _____

   _____

3. What is a *disability?* _____

4. A person with a disability is _____ .
   (Use the adjective form of the noun *disability*.)

D. **Dissecting a long medical word.** How many word parts are there in the word *electroencephalograph?* _____ What does the word mean? _____

E. **chir-**

1. What does the word part *chir-* mean? _____

2. What is *chiroplasty?* _____

3. What is *chiralgia?* _____

III. PRONOUNCING MEDICAL AND GENERAL WORDS

A. Look up each word below in your dictionary. Copy the pronunciation symbols (including the stress marks) next to the noun form given below. Then find the verb form, and write it down along with its pronunciation symbols. (*Note:* If your dictionary's symbols differ from the ones in this text, check the key to the symbols used in your dictionary.) Now say each noun/verb pair aloud.

NOUNS	SYMBOLS	VERBS	SYMBOLS
disability			
inhalation			
interpretation			
resuscitation			
supervision			

B. In the following words, both of the underlined vowels are pronounced. Say these words aloud.

alleviate [ie]   electrocardiograph [io]

podiatrist [ɑɪə]   radioactive [io]

IV. USING NEW WORDS AND PHRASES

Use the following words in the sentences below. (*Note:* you will need to use one of the words twice.)

alleviate	paramedics	patient	revive	traumatic
inhale	patience	relieved	stabilized	X-rays

1. Last week I was with my cousin John when he had a very

   _____ experience. He died.

2. John was in a serious automobile accident, and, when the

   _____ arrived on the scene, John wasn't breathing.

3. They immediately began CPR in order to _____ him.

4. I had only minor injuries from the accident, but I almost had a heart attack from worrying about my cousin. I was so

   _____ when he finally began to

   _____ and exhale on his own.

5. After the paramedics got his vital signs _____, they drove John and me to a nearby hospital.

6. I was given some first-aid treatment in the emergency room and then released, but John needed more care. The emergency-room

   physician ordered some _____ to determine if John had broken any bones.

7. Then she gave John a painkiller to _____ his discomfort. After that, she told John that she wanted him to be admitted to the hospital for further observation.

8. John didn't like being a _____ in a hospital. He wanted to go home the next day.

9. I said to him, "Be _____. Let the doctors do some more tests to be sure that you have no internal injuries."

10. But John didn't have any _____ at all. He wanted to be discharged the next day, but the resident finally

persuaded him to stay one more day for further observation. I kidded him a little and said, "You know, for a fellow who died yesterday, you are very difficult to get along with."

V. CHECKING COMPREHENSION

Reread the paragraph(s) indicated at the beginning of each statement below. Then underline the correct word or phrase to complete each statement or to answer the question.

1. [¶1] The phrase *rely upon* means **(a)** hire; **(b)** depend on; **(c)** train.

2. [¶3] The phrase *in accordance with the doctor's orders* means **(a)** following the physician's instructions; **(b)** telling the doctor what should be done; **(c)** agreeing with the doctor's decisions.

3. [¶4] This paragraph implies (suggests but does not say directly) that an electrocardiograph is **(a)** painful; **(b)** usually administered by a physician; **(c)** not a life-threatening procedure.

4. [¶7] According to this paragraph, occupational therapists **(a)** help patients find jobs; **(b)** work with disabled patients; **(c)** get all of their training on the job.

5. [¶11] According to this paragraph, **(a)** there have been physician assistants (PAs) for centuries; **(b)** PAs must have a license; **(c)** PAs have less training than nurses.

6. [¶11–15] Which of the following cannot perform any surgery? **(a)** a podiatrist; **(b)** a physician assistant; **(c)** an optometrist.

7. [¶12] A patient who is stabilized **(a)** is in good health; **(b)** is probably not in immediate danger of dying; **(c)** needs cardiopulmonary resuscitation.

CHAPTER 8

First Aid
in Medical
Emergencies

Cardiopulmonary resuscitation (CPR), which combines artificial respiration and external heart massage, can save a victim's life in an emergency.

1. Medical problems do not always develop slowly. Sometimes there are emergencies. An emergency is a situation that requires immediate care to prevent greater harm to the patient. However, it is not always possible to get professional medical help right away, so it is important for everyone to be familiar with **first-aid** procedures.

2. The main objective of first aid is to save lives. Fortunately, most first-aid procedures are not complicated and can be performed by someone with a minimum of training. In all **emergency** cases, a doctor should be called as well as an ambulance, if necessary. A written log should be made stating what treatment was administered and when it was started and completed. This information will be important to the medical personnel who treat the patient later.

3. One of the most serious emergencies occurs when an individual has stopped breathing. This may be the result of **asphyxiation,** electrocution, drowning, a heart attack, or some other cause. After only four minutes without oxygen, brain damage is likely. To prevent brain damage or death, artificial respiration must be started immediately.

4. Before resuscitation is begun, the victim should be placed face-up on a hard, flat surface. Rough handling should be avoided due to possible **fractures** which could cause spine injury, paralysis, or other internal injuries. The primary considerations include restoration of breathing and heartbeat. Clothing should be loosened and foreign matter or vomit cleared from the mouth.

5. Cardiopulmonary resuscitation (CPR) of a patient involves two procedures. The first is getting oxygen into the blood by blowing air into the lungs. Mouth-to-mouth breathing is the most effective form of artificial respiration. In this method, the rescuer breathes into the victim's mouth and nose in a regular **rhythm,** about 12 to 15 times per minute for an adult and 20 times for a child. As the air enters the lungs, the chest will expand. The second procedure is the application of chest pressure to **compress** the heart and force blood into the circulatory system. Pressure is applied with the heels of the hands on the victim's chest in a rocking motion, about 60 times a minute. This routine should not be stopped for longer than a beat or two. Even if one is **fatigued,** it is important to continue resuscitation efforts until help arrives. If one is alone with a victim, breathing and massage must be alternated, but CPR is much easier and far more effective if performed by a team of two. Anyone can learn CPR in classes offered by the American Red Cross or by local fire departments. The more people who are trained to administer CPR, the more lives can be saved.

6. After cardiac and/or pulmonary **arrest,** the most critical emergency is severe bleeding (hemorrhaging), especially from a main artery. Pressure must be placed at the site of the bleeding, or a **tourniquet** must be

applied. Care must be taken, however, to loosen the pressure from time to time to prevent **gangrene** (death of body cells caused by insufficient blood supply).

7.   Another common emergency is choking on food. Since the victim cannot talk because of the blocked trachea, it is important that others recognize the danger of the situation and act promptly. A procedure known as the *Heimlich maneuver* is commonly used to unblock the trachea. The victim is clutched from behind, and the rescuer sharply presses with his clutched hands on the victim's chest until the foreign object is **impel**led out of the trachea, and the victim is able to breathe.

8.   A condition that accompanies many medical emergencies is shock. When a victim is in shock, the bodily tissues are not receiving an adequate supply of oxygen-containing blood. To identify a state of shock, touch the skin and note its color. Shock victims feel sweaty and look very pale. Test the pulse. Someone in shock has a weak, rapid pulse. Also, shock victims may be nauseous or even vomiting. Shock is always serious and can be fatal. The victim should be made to lie flat with the feet raised. No food or drink should be given. External bleeding should be controlled, and the victim should be kept warm and comfortable until help arrives. These measures will usually minimize the most severe effects of shock.

9.   Severe injuries to the head rank among the most serious emergencies. If the skull is fractured or a victim suffers a **concussion,** the brain can be irreparably damaged. Warning signs of damage include unconsciousness, excessive sleepiness, vomiting, severe headaches, paralysis, bleeding, irregular breathing, confusion, extremely low pulse rate, dilated eye pupils, and memory loss. No **sedatives,** alcohol, or pain medications should be given. Food and fluids should be kept to a minimum. The victim should be moved as little as possible until a physician determines that there is no injury to the spine. A physician should be consulted in all cases, even if the victim has apparently recovered.

10.   Neck and back injuries are equally serious. A broken back can result in paralysis if the spinal cord is damaged. A victim with a back injury should be moved as little as possible to avoid further injury, although first aid to restore breathing or to stop bleeding should be undertaken.

11.   A very common but usually less serious emergency is a broken bone. A bone may be broken (or *fractured*) in a variety of ways. In a simple or *closed* fracture, the bone fragments do not pierce the skin. If the bone ends come through the skin, the break is known as a compound or *open* fracture, and there is a greater risk of infection.

12.   If a fracture is suspected, it is best not to have the victim test it by putting pressure on it—by walking, for example. Assume that the bone is fractured, and **immobilize** it until medical help is available.

13. Fractures must be distinguished from sprains and strains. A *sprain* is an injury to the ligaments, tendons, and soft tissues in the region of a joint. A *strain* is a muscle injury from overexertion or stretching. It is often necessary to X-ray the area to determine what kind of injury has occurred because similar symptoms — swelling, pain, and tenderness — are common to all three injuries.

14. Small lacerations (cuts) and simple hematomas (bruises) are not usually serious, but some blood clots (also called hematomas) can be very serious. There are several kinds of cuts and bruises. A contusion is a bruise to the tissue under the skin. An abrasion is a skin wound caused by rubbing or scraping. A puncture is a deep wound made by a piercing object. Whenever the skin is broken, the wound should be cleaned well with soap and water to remove foreign objects and dirt. Then it should be disinfected with an **antiseptic.** If necessary, a tetanus shot or booster should be given, especially if it is a puncture wound. If a cut is extensive, a doctor will use stitches (sutures) to close it. Even if a wound is treated and heals properly, it may still leave a permanent scar. Increasing pain, tenderness, swelling, pus, or red streaks around a wound are all signs of infection, which should be treated with medication. An infection can also cause fever.

15. Burns can be as trivial as a simple cut or can be cause for real concern. Burns are classified as first, second, or third degree, depending on their severity. A first-degree burn, such as a mild sunburn, involves just the outer surface of the skin; second- and third-degree burns, indicated by swelling, blistering, and a charred black color, involve the tissue below the skin and occasionally even underlying organs. Third-degree burns destroy the ability of the affected epidermis layer to **regenerate,** and treatment may require skin **graft**ing. A first-degree burn can be treated with a cooling lotion or cream, but more serious burns require prompt medical attention and possibly hospitalization to avoid shock and **dehydration** and to relieve severe pain.

16. Many household chemicals such as ammonia, bleach, and dishwasher detergent furnish the potential for serious crises. The ingestion of these and other poisonous substances frequently creates emergencies, especially among young children. The **antidote** for each substance is different, so instructions on the container should be followed closely. In some cases, the victim should be forced to vomit; a medicine called *ipecac* should be given to the patient to induce vomiting. However, with some poisonous substances, vomiting is harmful. In any case, a doctor should be contacted. Many communities have poison control centers where information can be obtained by telephone as to the proper treatment for different poisonous substances. Households with children should keep that phone number handy in case of such an emergency.

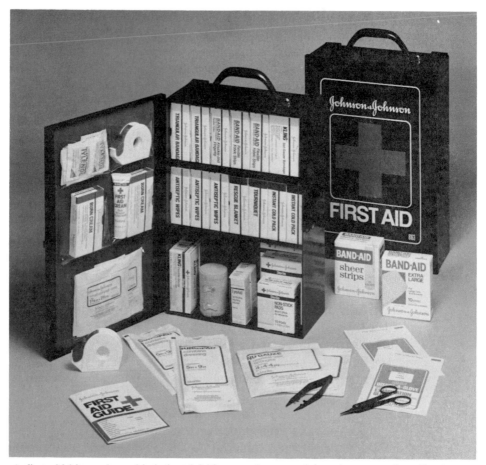

A first-aid kit, such as this industrial kit, contains essential equipment and medications for emergency situations. (*Courtesy of Johnson & Johnson*)

17.   Because speed is important in an emergency, it is helpful to have the emergency equipment and medications readily available in a first-aid kit. This kit should contain, at a minimum, a thermometer, antiseptic solution, an Ace bandage, equipment for making a splint, clean rags for a tourniquet, sterile absorbent cotton for cleaning wounds, and gauze pads with adhesive tape for bandaging them. A stethoscope, a sphygmomanometer for measuring blood pressure, a suture kit, and a tracheotomy kit are also useful to someone trained in their use.

18.   In any medical emergency, first aid is critical, but it is only the first step. Expert advice should be obtained while these measures are being taken. Many communities have mobile emergency medical vehicles operated by trained paramedics, who can render first aid beyond what the **layman** can do until the patient can be seen by a physician.

SPECIAL TERMS

Words Relating to Emergency Conditions

arrest — stop. A cardiac or pulmonary arrest refers to the cessation of heart-beat or breathing.

asphyxiation — loss of consciousness caused by insufficient oxygen in the blood. If the condition continues, permanent damage may result to the brain, heart, and other organs, and death may occur.

concussion — an injury to the brain, sufficient to cause impairment of brain function, at least temporarily, resulting from a blow to the head.

dehydration — excessive loss of water from the body.

fracture — a break, especially of a bone.

Words Relating to Treatment

antidote — a substance that neutralizes poisons or their effects.

antiseptic — chemical applied topically to the skin to kill harmful bacteria near and in the site of a wound.

compress — exert physical pressure upon something (to squeeze or press together). In the case of heart compression, the organ is pressed in to force the blood out of it and into the circulatory system.

first aid — treatment given a patient immediately following an emergency to prevent further injury or damage until professional medical care can be obtained.

graft — transferring tissue from one situs (position) of an organism to another situs in the same (or a different) organism with the expectation that the tissue will attach to it and become permanent, living tissue at the new situs. Skin grafts are common procedures whereby healthy skin is surgically removed from one part of the body and transferred to another part of the body, where the skin tissue has been damaged by burning or disease.

immobilize — prevent movement. After a fracture, the affected limb is placed in a cast or splint so that the bone will not move out of place. Immobilization is necessary first to prevent further injury to an unset bone and then to preserve the set fracture until it has healed.

sedative—a drug used to relax a person or render a person unconscious.

tourniquet—a device consisting of a flexible band that can be placed over a limb, and a lever which is placed inside of the band. The band is tightened by turning the lever, cutting off the blood circulation to the limb in order to stop bleeding at a source above the tourniquet. Because it completely shuts off circulation, a tourniquet must be loosened from time to time to prevent permanent damage to the tissue.

Other Medical Vocabulary

emergency—a condition which requires immediate attention to prevent serious damage or injury.

fatigue—loss of strength or energy usually caused by overexertion, insufficient sleep, or illness.

gangrene—death of tissue resulting from inadequate blood supply.

impel—move an object with force. By pressing forcefully on the chest, an object blocking the trachea can be forced out through the mouth.

layman—a person who is not trained as a professional. For example, a person who performs first aid but does not work in the medical field is a layman.

regenerate—grow again. In the human body, cells die and new ones replace them; this process is called regeneration.

rhythm—movement at regular time intervals. The heartbeat creates a rhythm of steady beats, each separated by the same amount of time.

VOCABULARY PRACTICE

1. When a child falls down and scrapes the top layer of skin on the knees, does the child need an antiseptic or an antidote?

2. When you compress something with your hands, do you push on it or pull it?

3. Richard was in an automobile accident and temporarily lost his memory. Did he have a compression or a concussion?

4. When there is an auto accident, who usually gives first aid—the accident victim, a physician, a police officer, or a paramedic?

5. What is a tourniquet used for?

6. If a tourniquet is kept tight for a long time, what damage might result?

7. Can you see any connection between the word *arrest* as it is used in medicine and as it is used in law enforcement?

8. Under what conditions is a person likely to get dehydrated? What can be done about it?

9. Should everyone be trained in first aid? Why?

10. What first-aid procedures would you follow if you suspected that an accident victim had fractured an arm?

11. What is the best treatment for fatigue?

12. Give some examples of medical emergencies.

13. If a physician administers a sedative to a patient, how is the patient likely to feel?

14. When the heart is functioning normally, it beats with a steady

    _____.

15. Sarah swallowed some floor polish! Call the poison control center

    and ask for the _____.

EXERCISES

I. DISCUSSING MEDICAL MATTERS

1. Have you ever administered first aid to a person who had had an accident or suddenly become ill? What did you do? Did the patient recover?

2. Have you ever needed first aid? Tell why, and tell what was done. What kinds of first aid have you administered to yourself?

3. Sometimes well-meaning but uninformed people do more harm than good when they try to administer first aid to an accident victim. Give some examples of the *wrong* things to do in various emergency situations.

4. What are some different kinds of accidental injuries to the skin? Give both the medical and common names, and discuss treatments.

II. ANALYZING WORDS AND WORD PARTS

A. Discuss the meaning of the phrase *foreign body*. How does this meaning relate to the common meanings of the individual words?

B. Write the meanings of the words *suscitate* and *resuscitate*.

_____   _____

What does a resuscitator do? _____

C. What is the Latin derivation (original meaning) of the word *emerge?* Check in a medical or general dictionary.

_____

How does this relate to the word *emergency?*

_____

D. What are the meanings of the two word parts in the word *immobile?*

_____   _____

What does the word *mobility* mean?

_____

What are the meanings of the two word parts in *automobile?*

_____   _____

E. What are the meanings of the three word parts in *dehydration?*

_____   _____   _____

III. PRONOUNCING MEDICAL AND GENERAL WORDS

A. **Pronouncing noun/verb pairs.** Often, an English word can be used as either a noun or a verb with no spelling change. Sometimes, however, the pronunciation changes. The common pattern is that the noun is stressed on the first syllable and the verb on the second. Say these words aloud, following the stress marks:

Nouns | *Verbs*

arrest′ | arrest′ (no change)

com′press | compress′

con′sole | console′

con′tents | content′

in′sult | insult′

Which noun/verb pairs have the same meanings? Which don't?

B. Pronounce the following words aloud, by reading the pronunciation symbols:

abrasion [əbreˈʒən] | television [tɛˈləvɪʒən]

physician [fɪzɪˈʃən] | laceration [læsɚeˈʃən]

Note the difference between the sounds [ʃ] and [ʒ].

C. Pronounce the following columns of words. Note the three different vowel sounds of the letter *y*. (When *y* appears at the beginning of a word, it has a consonant sound, as in *year*.)

[ɪ]		[aɪ]	[i]
asphyxiation	physician	dehydration	emergency
oxygen	rhythm	supply	injury
paralysis	system	underlying	

D.   Read the following sentences aloud. Be sure to pronounce the sounds [tʃ] and [ʃ] differently.

1. This child is choking on a piece of hard cheese.

2. You should put a blanket on that patient who is in shock so that she doesn't get chilled.

IV. USING NEW WORDS AND PHRASES

A.   Underline the correct word to complete each sentence below.

1. When you play tennis on a hot summer day and perspire a lot, your body may become **(a)** regenerated; **(b)** immobilized; **(c)** impelled; **(d)** dehydrated.

2. If you fall down a flight of stairs, a bone in your arm or leg may become **(a)** fractured; **(b)** fatigued; **(c)** sedated; **(d)** impelled.

3. Asphyxiation leads to pulmonary **(a)** graft; **(b)** arrest; **(c)** sedation; **(d)** rhythm.

4. A tourniquet is used to control **(a)** bleeding; **(b)** breathing; **(c)** vomiting; **(d)** gangrene.

5. An antiseptic is used to **(a)** counteract the effect of a poison; **(b)** kill germs; **(c)** cause gangrene; **(d)** compress the lungs.

6. In general, first-aid procedures are administered in order to **(a)** save the rescuer's life or minimize the rescuer's injuries; **(b)** save the victim's life or minimize the victim's injuries; **(c)** minimize the number of emergencies that occur; **(d)** increase the victim's discomfort and danger.

B.   Match each verb below with the meaning that it usually has in a medical setting.

1. accompany   _____ put

2. administer; render   _____ give (first aid, etc.)

3. assume   _____ go with

4. consult   _____ recognize differences

5. determine   _____ cause

6. distinguish   _____ reduce (make less)

7. induce   _____ keep something from happening

8. minimize   _____ regain health after illness (get well)

9. place   _____ conclude; decide

10. prevent   _____ suppose; believe

11. recover   _____ ask for someone's opinion or advice

12. suspect   _____ believe something is true because of good evidence

V. CHECKING COMPREHENSION

Reread the paragraph indicated at the beginning of each statement below. Then underline the correct word or phrase to complete each sentence.

1. [¶3–5] Artificial respiration (a) is a temporary substitute for the victim's normal breathing; (b) is administered to cause asphyxiation; (c) must be administered by two people.

2. [¶4] "Rough handling should be _avoided_. . . ." This statement tells the rescuer (a) to handle the patient gently; (b) not to move the patient at all; (c) to shake the patient vigorously to stimulate breathing.

3. [¶5–6] According to these paragraphs, in emergency medical treatment, two common uses of pressure are (a) to slow down blood circulation and to increase bleeding; (b) to stimulate circulation and to control bleeding; (c) to cause pulmonary and cardiac arrest.

4. [¶8] The medical condition known as _shock_ is always caused by (a) electricity; (b) danger or disappointment; (c) an inadequate supply of oxygen in the blood.

5. [¶11–13] A fracture always involves injury to (a) a bone; (b) a muscle and a bone; (c) ligaments and tendons.

6. [¶13] In this paragraph, the word _tenderness_ means (a) kindness; (b) pain when touched or pressed; (c) gentleness and affection.

7. [¶16] An antidote is needed after someone swallows (a) oxygen; (b) poison; (c) a sedative.

8. [¶18] In this paragraph, the word _critical_ means (a) an unkind remark; (b) needed to avoid a dangerous result; (c) optional.

CHAPTER 9

High-Tech Medicine and its Consequences

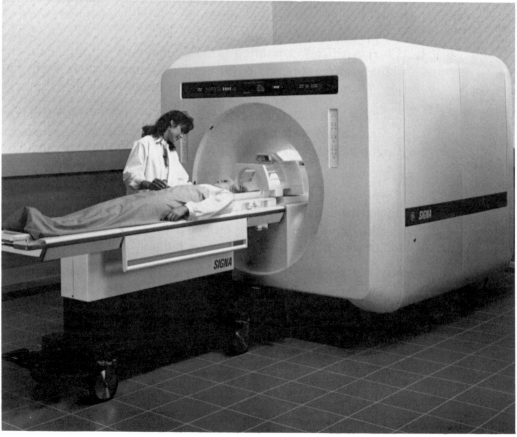

A Magnetic Resonance Imaging (MRI) system allows doctors to study virtually any portion of the human anatomy. (*Courtesy of GE Medical Systems*)

1. Chapter 8 discussed emergency medical procedures performed at the site of the emergency, before the patient reaches a hospital. In the hospital (and sometimes even before arrival there) high-tech equipment helps to save lives and minimize injury. To find out how **high technology** aids in emergency care as well as in medical diagnosis and treatment in general, let's tag along with Eva, a physician assistant (PA), as she tours a large hospital. Her guide is Henry, an emergency medical technician (EMT). Their first stop is a small room, where Gus, another EMT, is taking notes on the words and numbers flashing on a video display. "What's going on?" Eva asks.

2. "Well," says Gus, gesturing at the screen, "this is a readout of what one of our ambulances is doing. Right now Unit 3–2 (that's the second ambulance based here at South General) is transporting a forty-year-old woman injured in a motor vehicle accident with Code 3 (that's emergency lights and sirens). It looks like she's got low blood pressure and a fast pulse — probably shock. She's got a broken leg, too."

3. "Just think. These days we can make a diagnosis before we even see the patient. Aren't we wonderful?"

4. Henry asks, "Do you want to see the **Intensive Care Unit**? That's where most emergency transports end up if they aren't DOA (dead on arrival)."

5. As a patient lies by an array of equipment, the intensive-care nurse describes the ICU to Henry and Eva, as they stand in the doorway of a glass cubicle, one of a row of ten. "Monitoring of basic vital functions is completely automatic," she points out. "The **Swan-Ganz catheter** measures the outflow of the heart, that screen shows pressures, and that's the computer-calculated cardiac output. The blood pressure is measured from another catheter in an artery. Then the computer also has data on urine from a catheter in the bladder. The amount of fluid going into the patient's veins from the IV bottles over there is controlled by the computer. Because the patient's respiratory ability is compromised, there's an **endotracheal tube** connected to the respirator by a plastic hose, and the computer programs the respirator breathing cycles. You can see, there isn't much left to chance."

6. As Eva watches, the student nurse sitting beside the patient reaches out and gently wipes the sweat off his brow with a damp cloth. "I wonder which is more important, the computer or the nurse's hand," Eva remarks.

7. "Tell me about this part of the hospital," says Eva as they walk into a crowded hallway.

8. "This area we're passing is the CCU (**Cardiac Care Unit**). And down this hallway is the diagnostic services wing," says Henry. "It contains all sorts of X-ray equipment including the **Magnetic Resonance Imaging** (MRI) and **CT scanner.** CT means *Computerized Tomography.* I guess you know about that."

9.   "Yes," says Eva. "It's the machine that makes a picture which looks like a slice through the body."

10.   "It's fascinating," says Henry. "You can see a blood **clot** on the brain or a **tumor** in the abdomen, all without any surgery and in ten minutes or so. And there is **ultrasonography**, too," he continues. "It lets you examine a **fetus** or look at the internal movements of a beating heart."

11.   "One picture is worth a thousand words," says Eva.

12.   "Better yet," says Henry, "one picture can save a human life."

*   *   *

13.   High-tech equipment has been accused of causing the greatly increased cost of medical care. True, the equipment is expensive. But sometimes high-tech procedures save money by curing patients faster and by shortening hospital stays. Most important, high-tech equipment often enables physicians to prolong the active lives of patients, and it's impossible to put a price tag on the value of that.

14.   One impressive high-tech procedure is stereotaxis (precise, three-dimensional imaging), used for both diagnosis and treatment. Stereotaxis was introduced in 1950 as a means of treating people with Parkinson's disease. Today, thanks to CT scanning, MRI, and special stereotactic instruments, the technology is being used successfully to locate, biopsy, and treat brain tumors. **Stereotactic radiosurgery** is especially useful in treating tumors that are very deep and/or difficult to reach. This procedure involves three steps. First, the precise location of the tumor is determined. Next, under local anesthesia, a biopsy is performed through a very small opening. Finally, the tumor is treated, sometimes by radioactive **implants** around the tumor, sometimes by a single high dose of radiation.

15.   Another high-tech device—the **laser**—has enabled surgeons to dispense safer, less painful, more accurate treatment. Lasers have been used on the human body from head to foot, treating everything from major eye problems to minor foot problems. The word *laser* is an acronym for *light amplification by stimulated emission of radiation*. The very first laser was produced in 1959. Lasers have been used in eye surgery since the early 1970s. Today, various kinds of lasers are used in many medical specialties including gynecology, gastroenterology, otolaryngology, neurosurgery, and dermatology. Lasers have been used to remove appendixes (with only a small incision) and to do biopsies.

16.   In general, lasers operate by creating an intense amount of light and energy which is then converted into heat and used to control bleeding or destroy diseased tissue. Different types of rays treat different problems. For example, the different color beams of the argon laser are used to treat diabetes-related eye problems, retinal tears, and macular degeneration. A

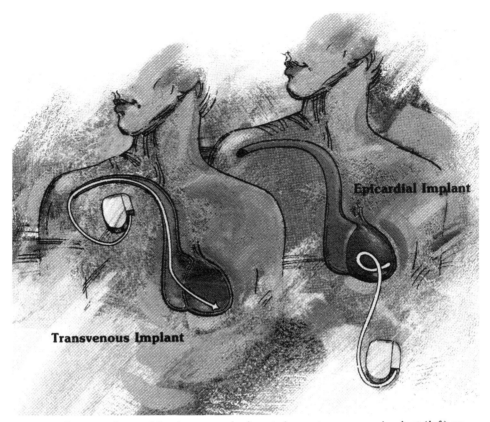

A pacemaker, one form of implant, may be inserted as a *transvenous implant* (*left*) or, where the patient wishes to avoid a scar in the shoulder area, as an *epicardial implant* (*right*). (*Courtesy of Medtronic, Inc.*)

high-energy neodynium laser allows surgeons to shrink tumors in the lungs, esophagus, stomach, rectum, and bladder.

17.   Many physicians predict that the laser will be the chief medical tool of the future, while others warn that it is overused to perform procedures that could be handled just as well by older methods. Some benefits are obvious: in many cases, the laser has simplified surgical procedures, reduced medical complications, and cut costs by enabling surgical patients to go home after only a short hospital stay or a one-day visit to an outpatient clinic. Patients who have had laser surgery are the biggest fans of the technology because they experience less pain and recover more quickly than patients treated for the same problem by more conventional surgery.

18.   But lasers are not the last word in high-tech surgery. For many years now, people have been building **robots.** In the not-too-distant future, robots may be returning the favor by helping to rebuild people. In 1990, a robot named *Robodoc* performed a successful hip replacement on a dog

named Mindy. The computerized robot, programmed with the exact dimensions of the implant, cut an opening in the thigh exactly the right size for the artificial joint. Because of the precision that a robot can deliver, robots will likely soon be utilized to operate on human beings. Perhaps they'll begin as orthopedic robosurgeons, but, once they're admitted into the human hospital world, who knows what other surgical talents they might display?

19.   Other innovative medical procedures are in experimental or beginning stages and include major surgery on fetuses, organ transplants from living donors, and the development of artificial blood.

20.   Doctors have been operating on fetuses since the early 1980s, performing relatively simple procedures such as repairing urinary tract blockages or draining fluid from the brain. But in 1990, a team of British doctors performed the first successful **prenatal** heart operation on a fetus in the last trimester of development. The surgeons corrected a heart valve defect with a tiny balloon catheter guided into place with the help of an ultrasound **scan.**

21.   Organ transplants (most commonly of the kidney, heart, or liver) from cadavers have been quite successful, and the general public has come to view them as almost routine. In 1990, surgeons began performing liver transplants from a living donor. The procedure involves taking a part of the liver from a close relative of the patient (usually from parent to child) and implanting it in the patient. In its new site, the liver then grows to normal adult size along with the patient. The antirejection drug cyclosporin has greatly reduced the chance of rejection of these donor organs, so more surgeons and patients are now willing to try the procedure.

22.   Artificial blood is no longer just for gangster movies. A new blood substitute (a fluorinated hydrocarbon emulsion chemically similar to Teflon) can carry oxygen to cells in much the same way as the hemoglobin in human blood does. While still in the experimental stages, artificial blood is yet another possible high-tech lifesaver of the future.

*   *   *

23.   The technology of modern medicine has, of course, prolonged human life and, in general, reduced human suffering. However, along with increasing power have come many new questions—medical, legal, and social. These are just some of them:

(a)   Who is to pay for the expensive, high-tech medical care that modern medicine has to offer?

(b)   As medical care becomes more and more complex and specialized, patients find themselves consulting a different doctor for each ailment.

What, then, happens to the doctor-patient relationship, and which medical practitioner assesses the medical needs of the total person?

(c) Today, either sophisticated ultrasound scans or **amniocentesis** can be used to check a fetus for serious abnormalities. But when prospective parents have that information, sometimes they must make a painful moral decision. When is a deformity serious enough to warrant aborting the fetus?

(d) Now that it is possible to transplant the human **embryo,** a baby can have two mothers—the birth mother (who carried the fetus) and the genetic mother (who provided the egg). Which one is the "real" mother? Courts of law sometimes have to answer this tough question. In a battle for custody, who should be the winner?

(e) When high-tech medical care can "save" extremely premature infants only to send parents home with seriously handicapped babies, who is to decide when medical care is appropriate?

(f) When transplanted organs can save lives, but the number of donor organs is limited, who decides which patients to save?

(g) When medical care can keep terminally ill people alive and suffering much longer than patients wish to live, who is to define the doctor's role in assisting the patient to "die with dignity"?

(h) Nowadays, special equipment can keep people "alive" (that is, with heartbeat and respiration continuing) long after their brains are capable of human functions. Who is to define death and determine when it is ethical to discontinue treatment? Many physicians believe that the most conclusive evidence of death is brain death, the absence of all electrical activity in the brain (according to an electroencephalograph) for 24 hours. However, not everyone would agree that, after that time, life support systems on a **comatose** patient can legally be removed. Many people, concerned about being kept "alive" in a vegetative state, are signing *living wills,* legal documents stating under what circumstances high-tech lifesaving measures should be abandoned and the patient allowed to die. Some sign a document called a *power of attorney,* which authorizes a designated relative or friend to make medical decisions regarding the person's life or death if the person ever becomes too ill to make rational decisions. However, since many people do not have such documents, the medical dilemma caused by comatose patients "living" for many years remains with us.

(i) Now that medical science is keeping people alive longer, who is to support the increasing numbers of elderly, chronically ill people?

24. Clearly, the power of modern medicine is a mixed blessing. While it prolongs human life, in doing so it sometimes also prolongs the suffering of ill people and their families. Like any other powerful tool, high-tech medical care must be used with discretion. Although the human body is often compared to a machine, there are important differences: a machine does not feel physical or mental anguish and does not cry out in agony. We want our automobile to last as long as possible; we don't have to ask our broken car if it wants to be repaired and sent back on the road again. But despite "miracle drugs," computers, lasers, and so on, health care workers are still primarily dealing with people. With people, the goal must be to increase not only the quantity of life but also the quality. That is the dual challenge facing contemporary medicine. It is, on a higher level, the same challenge health care workers have always faced.

SPECIAL TERMS

Medical Equipment and Instruments

CT (computerized tomography) **scanner** — a machine for producing computer-generated X-ray photographs around an area of the body. This produces a cross-sectional view of the site.

endotracheal tube — a tube inserted into a patient's trachea to keep an airway open. One of its main uses is to insure an open airway when general anesthesia is administered during surgery.

implant — a device inserted into the interior of a living organism for the purpose of diagnosis or treatment. A pacemaker, used to regulate the heartbeat, is an example of an implant.

laser — a narrowly focused, high-energy beam of light. Lasers are used for cutting and for cauterizing. Surgery by laser is more accurate, heals more quickly, and causes less bleeding than conventional surgery.

Magnetic Resonance Imaging (MRI) — a noninvasive method of viewing internal body structures (including soft tissue) by the use of a strong magnetic field, radio waves, and computers. Patients are placed upon a flat bed and through a tunnel-like device where scans are made of the area involved. There is ordinarily no discomfort to the patient from the process.

robot—a mechanical device operated by computer or remote control which can perform some of the functions of a human. Robots are used where extreme accuracy is necessary or in situations that would endanger a human, such as areas of high radiation.

scan—a device for measuring the concentration of a radioactive substance introduced into an area of the body for diagnostic purposes.

stereotactic radiosurgery—a surgical technique involving CT scans, MRI, and special computer equipment to precisely locate, identify, and biopsy tissue within the head. If necessary and possible, the patient is treated by radiation, radioactive implants, or surgery. Because the area can be viewed in three dimensions, diagnosis and treatment can be more precise than with other methods. Exploratory surgery employing this method can be done under local anesthetic.

Swan-Ganz catheter—a hollow tube (catheter) inserted into the patient's body which allows measurement of pressure within the vascular system near or in the heart. It is also called a pulmonary artery catheter or PA line.

ultrasonography—use of very high frequency sound waves directed precisely and controlled by computer to assemble an image of the shape and movement of parts of the human body.

Words Relating to Human Reproduction

amniocentesis—removal of fluid from the amniotic sac by hypodermic needle. The contents of the fluid can be analyzed to identify any abnormalities in the fetus. The gender of the fetus can also be identified by this procedure.

embryo—the very earliest stages of development of a fertilized ovum. In humans, the embryonic period is the first two months after conception.

fetus—in humans, the child in utero from the third month until birth.

prenatal—relating to the time between conception of an embryo and birth of the child.

Other Medical Vocabulary

Cardiac Care Unit (CCU) – an intensive care unit specifically designed for cardiac patients.

clot – thick coagulated mass of blood. Clotting is caused by platelets and numerous special proteins found in the blood. Blood clotting prevents uncontrolled bleeding, but it can be dangerous if it blocks the circulation.

comatose – an abnormally deep stupor caused by illness or injury. A person in this state cannot be aroused by external stimuli.

high technology – the use of modern, highly sophisticated equipment and/or knowledge to solve problems.

Intensive Care Unit (ICU) – special section of the hospital in which intensive nursing and high technology are used to monitor and support life in critical situations.

tumor – an abnormal growth of tissue, usually of unknown cause. Tumors are generally classified as benign (not cancerous) or malignant (cancerous).

VOCABULARY PRACTICE

1. Name three high-tech pieces of equipment that involve the use of computers and that create images of the interior of the human body.

2. Is an endotracheal tube high-tech equipment?

3. What kinds of emergencies would an endotracheal tube and a pacemaker be used to deal with?

4. What two medical tasks can a laser do?

5. What are three advantages of laser surgery over conventional surgery?

6. Why would a robot be useful in some types of surgery?

7. What does a Swan-Ganz catheter measure?

8. What is another name for the Swan-Ganz catheter?

9. What kinds of waves are used by sonography and by MRI?

10. Which develops first—the fetus or the embryo?

11. What are some possible reasons why a patient becomes comatose?

12. What are the two main categories of tumors?

13. Which high-tech diagnostic instruments involve the use of a scanner?

14. To what area of a hospital would a heart attack victim be taken for initial care?

15. What are three advantages to the patient of the use of stereotactic surgery?

EXERCISES

I. DISCUSSING MEDICAL MATTERS

1. Have you ever had (or observed) an MRI test or a CT scan? If so, describe the procedure.

2. What is a laser, and how is it used by physicians?

3. Name some illnesses that can be diagnosed more accurately because of high-tech equipment.

4. What kinds of patients will you find in the ICU and CCU of a hospital?

5. Do you believe that physicians should help terminally ill patients "die with dignity"? What risks does such a policy entail?

II. ANALYZING WORDS AND WORD PARTS

A. Write the meanings of the word parts in each word below. Then write a definition of each word.

stereotaxis: _____   _____

_____

_____

tomography: _____   _____

_____

_____

B. Write the words for each set of initials below.

   1. CT _____

   2. DOA _____

   3. EMT _____

   4. ICU _____

   5. MRI _____

   6. PA _____

C. Complete each word or phrase in the column on the right to make a word or phrase that means the opposite of a word or phrase in the column on the left.

   1. high dose   anti _____

   2. input   im _____

   3. maximize   low _____

   4. personal   mini _____

   5. rejection   out _____

   6. underused   over _____

III. PRONOUNCING MEDICAL AND GENERAL WORDS

   A. **Stress changes.** Pronounce each noun / adjective pair below, noting the stress changes.

   de′fect; defec′tive   exper′iment; experimen′tal

   B. **Compound vowel sounds.** Say the following words aloud. Pronounce the underlined vowels as two separate sounds, as shown in the bracketed symbols after each word.

amniocentesis [io]   endotracheal [iə]

biopsy [aɪɑ]   radiation [ie]

embryo [io]   stereotaxis [io]

C. Pronounce the following boxed words aloud. Pronounce the letter *u* as shown in the symbol above each column.

[yu]		[ə]	[u]
calculate future		adult	fluid
computer human		fetus	occlude
cubicle use		rectum	reduce
document unit		ultrasound	include

D. Pronounce the following words with the letters *ur*. The sound is [ɚ] or [yɚ].

cure   measure   surgeon   urine

In which two words is the sound [yɚ]?

E. Practice contrasting the sounds [f] and [p] in these words.

fetus / Peter   pain / paint / faint   foot / put

practice / fracture   fan / pan   pressure / fresh air

people / feeble   price / fright

F. Pronounce these words aloud: fatal / fetal.

IV. USING NEW WORDS AND PHRASES

A. Match the opposites by writing the numbers on the lines.

1. artificial   _____ reduce

2. complicate   _____ simplify

3. experimental   _____ real

4. general   _____ local

5. increase   _____ fluid; liquid

6. precise   _____ enlarge; expand

7. prolong   _____ conventional

8. shrink   _____ shorten the time; speed up

9. solid   _____ approximate

B.   Discuss the meanings of the following phrases used in this chapter.

1. cardiac output (¶5)

2. die with dignity (¶23 g)

3. left to chance (¶5)

4. vegetative state (¶23 h)

5. the last word (¶18)

6. living will (¶23 h)

7. return the favor (¶18)

8. chronically ill (¶23 i)

V. CHECKING COMPREHENSION

Underline the correct phrase to complete each statement below.

1. In ¶6, Eva is suggesting that **(a)** the personal touch may be as important as high-tech equipment; **(b)** machines are replacing people in providing medical care; **(c)** a machine could wipe a person's forehead.

2. According to ¶15, an acronym is **(a)** a word created from the first letter of each word in a phrase; **(b)** an abbreviation; **(c)** a kind of laser.

3. By carefully rereading ¶19 and studying the word in context, you can conclude that the word *innovative* means **(a)** a change; **(b)** high technology; **(c)** conventional.

4. ¶20 suggests that a *fetus* is **(a)** an unborn baby; **(b)** an infant; **(c)** a heart defect.

5. After reading ¶21, you can assume that rejection of a donor organ is **(a)** good for the patient; **(b)** harmful to the donor; **(c)** harmful to the patient.

6. According to this chapter, which of the following is not high-tech medical care? **(a)** laser surgery; **(b)** ultrasonography; **(c)** a biopsy.

7. In ¶23 h, the word *alive* is in quotation marks because **(a)** the text is repeating the exact words of a speaker; **(b)** the authors don't believe that a person in a vegetative state is fully alive as a human being is meant to be; **(c)** the word *alive* is being used as slang in this sentence.

8. According to this chapter, in general, high-tech medicine has **(a)** brought many benefits and created some problems; **(b)** greatly decreased the cost of medical care; **(c)** done more harm than good by increasing human suffering.

Review Exercises (Chapters 6-9)

I. Match each medical problem with an appropriate treatment.

1. abrasion	_____ amputation
2. cardiac arrest	_____ antidote
3. choking	_____ antiseptic
4. dehydration	_____ antiseptic and tetanus shot
5. fracture	_____ skin graft
6. gangrene	_____ Heimlich maneuver
7. ingestion of poison	_____ resuscitation
8. puncture wound	_____ splint; cast
9. third degree burn	_____ fluids

II. Write the meaning of each word part below. Use a dictionary for help.

1. dis- _____

2. intra- _____

3. -oxia _____

4. para- _____

5. -septic _____

6. -stalsis _____

7. -tomy _____

8. trans- _____

9. -trophy _____

10. viv- _____

III. Circle the correct answers.

1. Which two of the following are not surgical instruments?

scalpel   catheter   retractor   drape   forceps

2. Which of the following is not an abnormal condition?

ambulation   shock   dehydration   asphyxiation   paralysis

3. Which three of the following are not surgical procedures?

hysterectomy   herniorrhaphy   ultrasonography   hypertension

pulmonary arrest

4. Which three of the following can be used to help a physician or a technician make a diagnosis?

robot   centrifuge   laser   MRI   tourniquet

IV. Match each word with the word or phrase that means the same.

1. antiseptic   _____ stitch (to sew up a surgical incision or a wound)

2. asphyxiation   _____ treatment

3. excise   _____ broken bone

4. fatigue   _____ to cut out; remove surgically

5. fracture   _____ to cut into with a sharp instrument

6. hematoma   _____ a feeling of tiredness

7. immobilize   _____ germ-killer

8. incise   _____ bruise

9. laceration   _____ suffocation; obstruction of the air passages

10. resuscitate   _____ to prevent movement

11. suture   _____ to revive

12. therapy   _____ a wound or irregular tear of the flesh

International Phonetic Alphabet

In accordance with common practice and for reasons of simplification, these minor changes in symbols have been introduced. [ə] and [ɚ] are used in this book for both stressed and unstressed syllables. [y] is used instead of IPA [j]. [ɑ] is used instead of IPA [a].

CONSONANTS

[p] – pie, hope, happy

[b] – bell, bite, globe

[f] – fine, office

[v] – vest, of, have

[k] – keep, can, book

[g] – go, get, egg

[l] – let, little, lay

[m] – man, must, dime

[n] – no, down, ton

[ŋ] – sing, ringing

[w] – water, we, one

[θ] – thin, three, path

[ð] – they, then, other

[s] – see, sat, city

[z] – zoo, does, is

[ʃ] – shoe, ship, action

[ʒ] – usual, garage

[tʃ] – chance, watch

[dʒ] – June, edge

[r] – red, rich, write

[y] – you, yes, million

[h] – he, hat, who

[t] – ten, to, meet

[d] – do, did

VOWELS AND DIPHTHONGS

[ɪ] – it, did, build

[i] – me, see, people

[ɛ] – end, let, any

[æ] – cat, bat, laugh

[ɑ] – army, father, hot

[ɔ] – all, caught, long

[ʊ] – book, full, took

[u] – too, move, fruit

[ə] – cup, soda, infant

[ɚ] – her, work, bird

[e] – say, they, mail

[o] – old, coal, sew

[ɑɪ] – dry, eye, buy

[ɔɪ] – toy, boy, soil

[ɑʊ] – cow, our, house

Index of Special Terms